Thorns Have Roses

Ira David Welch

Copyright © 2024 by

IRA DAVID WELCH

ALL RIGHTS RESERVED. No part of this book may be reproduced or transmitted in any form by any means, electronic or mechanical, including photocopying and recording, or by any information storage and retrieval system, except as may be expressly permitted in writing from the author.

ISBN: 978-1-962905-50-3

Printed in the United States of America

Published by Writersclique.com

Dedication

To my family . . .

my wife, we have shared a lifetime together

  Marie

our sons and our daughters-in-law. They have enriched our lives beyond description

  Dave and Shauna   *Dan and Ali*

and especially our grandchildren . . .
They have given us the gift of the future

  Aiden   *Paige & Ryan*

Acknowledgments

Any author knows that no book comes to press with the contributions of the author alone. It is true for this book as well. My wife, Marie, has been a constant source of support, a sounding board, and an editor throughout. Thank you to Dr. Leslie McCarroll, a teammate, student, colleague, and now friend, for his thorough reading of a late draft and for his critical comments throughout. I am grateful to our son, Dan Welch, who agreed to create the painting for the cover. His artwork over the years has been a joy to his mother and me. I want to say a special Thank You to Fred Adams who has faithfully guided me through the entire process. I also want to thank the folks at Writer's Clique for their early encouragement and support through the publishing process. They were trustworthy guides all through the process. My appreciation also goes to those whose work I have quoted both in lengthy passages and for their stimulating thoughts that led to this final product. Finally, I pay tribute to my teachers, both formal and informal, who have instructed, guided, and supported me over these many years. I first met Dr. Richard Usher when I was an undergraduate. He was such an inspirational teacher that it prompted me to change my major from Business to Education. His influence led me into the fields of teaching, psychology, and counseling. Over the years, he evolved from teacher to colleague to friend. Dick and Mary, and their daughter, Tish, have become lifelong friends to Marie and me. I first met Fred and Anne Richards as graduate students at the University of Florida. From classmates, we have grown together into life companions and have taught together, written together, and grown together over the years. Dick and Mary and Fred and Anne are godparents to our son, Dan. It is difficult to imagine how my life would have been without these four people who command the purest love I have to give. During the publication of this book, my friend, Fred Richards, died at his home in Carrollton, GA. I mourn his death and the gap it places in my life. Finally, my students, too numerous to mention, have taught me, formed me, and opened windows to the future I am certain I would not have seen without their questions, arguments, and insistence that I clarify my thoughts. "Great Love" is a closing I learned from Novelist Pat Conroy, and it is the one I use with my family and close friends when I write to them. It is one which I offer to my students. It is the one I will use here.

> Great Love,
>
> Ira David Welch
>
> Denver, Colorado

PREFACE

I am quite an old man now. A startling fact, even to me, is that I have spent 75% of my life in the classroom. Of my four score years and three, fully 60 have been in the classroom as a student or a teacher. I taught 18-to-36-month-old toddlers in preschool for two years and then jokingly said I was kicked into higher education because they pay you according to the height of your students. I taught at the college or university level for more than 40 years. In preparation for that career, I spent 20 years as a student in classrooms from elementary school through a doctorate. Like other professions, being a student doesn't stop after one receives your final degree but continues through workshops, professional conventions, additional training, and even personal research into those puzzling questions of one's profession that still nag. When I retired from teaching, I was blessed to be invited upon occasion to give public talks on one subject or another. Quite a few of these were "sermons" presented at Unitarian-Universalist churches, mostly in Arkansas and Colorado. Some appear in this book, most notably the chapters Thorns Have Roses, Put Me in Coach, The Goldilocks Zone, Pray to God and Continue to Swim toward Shore, I Know a Way out of Hell, Would Jesus Wear a Rolex?, Five Smooth Stones, and With Mirth and Laughter. The other chapters include thoughts and ideas I have had over the years and ones that I think have some relevance for others. It is probably important here to tell the reader that I am not criticizing the ideas of others, nor am I suggesting that my ideas should supplant theirs. My hope lies more along the lines of informing, thinking out loud, and, perhaps, provoking thoughts and exploration. Since we live in Denver, Colorado, our daily newspaper is the Denver Post. The Founder of the Post was Fredrick G. Bonfils (1861-1933). He insisted that this motto, "There is no hope for the satisfied man," be displayed prominently on the Editorial Page of every issue. Aside from the masculine construction, it is a sentiment with which I agree. It is the history of humanity to push forward, to look over the next mountain, to cross the wide sea, or to capture an image on a cave wall, and even to leave the earth to explore space. As we look at the chapter "The Story of Us," for example, we find that what separated Homo Neanderthals from Homo Sapiens was the continued change in "technology" for the Homo Sapiens. For some reason, the Neanderthals, a successful and dominant species for 100,000 years, stalled in their innovation and modification of the tools they used. This a historical point to which we should pay careful attention. The rate of change is, perhaps, greater now than it has ever been. The lesson is that we have to keep looking not only at the technology but also at the social organizations, political strategies, and environmental concerns that will form our future. My hope in writing this book is that it encourages the reader to continue to push forward, and, as I write below, one of the major reasons for writing the book is as a message to our grandchildren. They are all young now. The oldest is just approaching high school. Their generation is, of course, the future. If they follow the wisdom of the Homo Sapiens Sapiens of years gone by, and by extension, some of the advice contained herein, then the future will be in very good hands. That is a hope I believe we all can share. I found upon retirement that I missed the classroom. I didn't miss the politics of university life, committee meetings, or grading student work. But, I did miss talking to people about ideas that matter to me. When I am asked to speak, it gives me the chance to actively spend time thinking about ideas. So, in a sense, it keeps me active mentally. This collection of thoughts are ones that I modestly think are ideas from which others may profit, learn, and, perhaps, even be inspired. This leads most directly to the major underlying reason I wrote and published this book. It is for our grandchildren: Paige, Ryan, and Aiden. They are the citizens of the future. I hope that whatever wisdom I have gathered through my long life will have some meaning to them, even aid them, as they move into the world of adulthood, undertake careers, and make the decisions that will form their world and the future. Carpe Diem et Carpe Futurum.

Table Of Contents

1

Thorns Have Roses 1

2

Miracles 19

3

Put Me In Coach 21

4

The Courage To Be Imperfect 39

5

The Hardiness Factor: How The Tough Get Going When The Going Gets Tough 51

6

The Goldilocks Zone, the Inverted "U" and the Secret to Contentment 61

7

Pray to God and Continue to Swim Toward Shore 71

8

Wishes 83

9

I Know a Way Out of Hell 85

10

Would Jesus Wear A Rolex? Poverty, Wealth And Our Spiritual Well Being 101

11

Five Smooth Stones 119

12

Enlightenment 137

13

The Secret to a Better World 139

14

Two Ducks – A Parable 151

15

The Lion Who Thought He Was a Sheep 153

16
The Pig Who Thought He Was a Dog 155

17
A Special Chapter For Teachers 157

18
The Story of Us 161

19
Transcendence 175

20
Liberty and Justice For All 177

21
Statistics and Gratitude 193

22
With Mirth And Laughter 197

23
"Civilization and Its Discontents":
Institutional Oppression and the
Authentic Society 211

24
Mountain Top 223
25
Hope, Optimism, and the Future 225
Epilogue 241
About The Author 249

1
THORNS HAVE ROSES

Talk to any Florist and he or she will tell you that roses have thorns. We all know that and we use it to teach ourselves that life comes with some cautions and not to be naive or gullible. Happiness can be fleeting. It is a truth, important to know, and at the same time, something of a dangerous knowledge, lest we become cynical and fearful of living, especially without its corresponding truth. Thorns have Roses.

Let me tell you a story. It is a bit personal since it involves someone I know. A young man of my acquaintance was employed with a national company that did what is described as Ligation Support – it involved all the printed material associated with a Trial and formatting it (at the time) into organized, indexed, and accessible notebooks for all the Officers of the Court (Plaintiff, Defense, Judge, Court

Recorder, and so forth) – this evolved into the electronic organization and storage of such material. He was quite good and successful in this field, but one morning – three days before Christmas – he came into work and was called into the Director's Office, where he was told that the company was going to "let him go." There would be a severance package, but his employment with the company would cease by the end of the year. He asked "why," of course, and the reason was that it had been determined by corporate that the office needed to reduce costs. Downsize in corporate language. He was their most productive account manager and, thus, the most expensive to the company. So, in the reasoning of the corporate world, I suppose it made sense to get rid of the most expensive employee even though he was their top producer. Just recently, I read that a noted TV Commentator was told a few days before Christmas that she would not be rehired. What is it about the corporate world that they seem to fire people just before Christmas? Well, the young man was devastated. Talking about it later, he called it "the worst day of my life." We talked it over, and he decided to take some time to figure out the next step in his life. He talked with some of his clients (all attorneys) and with some friends. In the legal world, there is an agreement certain types of employees have to sign called a "Non-Competition Agreement." Essentially, it means that if you stop working for a company, you agree not to join another company in the same field – so as not to carry business decisions, trade-craft, or even clients to the new firm. It turned out – in discussions with his attorney clients – that his company had made something of a mistake. It turned out that if the company "fires" you, then the "Non-Competition Agreement" is voided, and he wasn't required to abide by the terms of the agreement. He could be employed by a competitor. What he did instead was to form his own small company with several clients for whom he had previously been the account manager. His new company included himself, two technicians, and a dozen or so former clients. It was tight going in the early days, but within about 3 years, his company had 15 employees and was 4th in the city in terms of market share. Sweet Revenge. Later, he said of his "firing," "It was the best thing that ever happened to me."

Another personal story. There was a little girl named Tessie who stuttered badly as a child. She attended a play when she was about six years old and dreamed that she, one day, would be an actress, but her stuttering was a huge obstacle. Some years later, through the guidance and support of a high school drama teacher, who cast her in her first play, "Tea House of the August Moon," she overcame her stuttering, received a college scholarship, became a theater major, and ultimately performed on both the stage and in motion pictures, in more than 60 productions. She is my wife, Marie Therese. "Tessie," her mother called her. Thorns sometimes have Roses.

I've lived a long time now, and I know that if there is anything like a Law of Nature, it is that Life comes with tragedy. We don't have to do anything special. It is simply the case that life comes with sadness built in. Our life experience, reading, and entertainment all teach us this. One of the annual movie favorites at Christmas is "It's a Wonderful Life." The main character, George Bailey, is resentful and even suicidal about his life, which he views as wasted. You know the story: guardian angel Clarence is sent to save him. George learns that his life, far from being wasted, even though his early dreams had not been realized, has, in fact, been a life in which his family, his friends, in fact, his whole community, is a far better place than it would have been without him. It has been, indeed, "a wonderful life." Thorns have Roses.

Mark Taylor of Mattel Toys created Skeletor, one of the most successful action figures of all time. It's a frightening-looking "Bad Guy" with a skull for a face and muscles like a bodybuilder. One of the best 'bad guys" of the action figure genre. He was asked how he came up with the Skeletor creation, and he tells the story of going to an amusement park when he was a kid. He went into the House of Horrors and stepped on a plank, and out popped a skeleton hanging from a rope. It frightened him so badly he fled the scene and had nightmares for years. When it came time to create a villain to fight against He-Man, that childhood experience became the inspiration for the villain, Skeletor.

One of my colleagues years ago was quite a tall man, 6 feet 6 inches. He was a very accomplished basketball player in high school. He told me how he had been kidnapped by the Coach of a University and hidden in a motel so other coaches couldn't find him until after signing day when he committed to the university. He played for 4 years and was drafted by the Detroit Pistons. In the summer between his graduation and professional camp, both his knees "exploded," and he never played a moment of professional basketball. Instead, he went to graduate school, obtained his doctorate, and became a college professor and, from his perspective, a far more rewarding and fulfilling life.

I spent a great part of my professional life working with people dealing with the tragedies of life, including chronic disease, death, grief, and bereavement. I worked for many years with the Multiple Sclerosis Society of Colorado and worked with groups and individuals coping with MS. I remember in one support group a member said that after years of coping with MS, she had an odd sort of gratefulness for the disease in her life. She talked about her earlier life in which she described herself as a self-centered, demanding, and somewhat callous young woman without much regard for others. MS, she said, taught her compassion, care, and concern for others. Her pain contributed to the development of empathy for others, something, she said, she was certain would not have happened in her life unless she had to face the misfortunes she had.

Michael Landon starred in the movie, *The Loneliest Runner*, which was the story of Gene Orowitz, a high school student struggling with bed-wetting, whose mother tried to shame him by hanging his wet sheets out the window for all to see. He would run home every day to pull the sheets in before his friends could see them. He tried out for the track team, became a state champion, received a college scholarship, and went on to great acclaim as a runner. When asked to what he attributed his success as a runner, he said, "I guess I would have to thank my mother." Gene Orowitz changed his name to Michael Landon in this roughly autobiographical movie and went on to theatrical acclaim, especially in television programs such as *Bonanza, Little House on the Prairie, and Highway to Heaven*. Thorns have roses.

Maya Angelou, one of our strongest voices in contemporary literature and one whom any would point to as a role model would surprise them with her true life story. She was not a "golden child" blessed with early signs of her future success. She, in fact, had a childhood that would have more likely predicted disaster and shame. She has herself written about her experiences taking drugs. She had a baby when she was a teenager. She was, for a time, a prostitute and even acted as a madam for lesbian prostitutes. Somehow, out of these experiences, she found a way to give lies to the predictions and create another life – a life of wholesomeness and personal worth. She has traveled the path from teenage drug user and prostitute to Poet Laureate of the United States and a person well worth our respect. A real model that adversity can be overcome and a positive future created. Again, Thorns have roses.

Let's take a religious, theological turn here for a moment. I want to talk with you about Jesus - perhaps the best example of a positive outcome from a tragic event in history. At least positive from the point of view of Christians for whom the torture and death of Jesus, the Christ, is their personal salvation. Jesus Christ is a savior from eternal punishment and a giver of eternal life. For this theological group, there is no way other than the death of Christ for a person to enter heaven. Quote: "If Jesus never was mocked, persecuted, whipped, beaten, or lied about, we would never have escaped our due punishment in hell." Did you ever play that game where you speculate about "What If?" What if you could change the past? What if you could return to 1st-century Palestine? What if you could save Jesus from his torture and death? Would you? I used to belong to a religious group for whom I am fairly certain the members would vote "no" they would not save Jesus. Jesus's death was necessary to obtain God's forgiveness. I belong to a religious group now, the Unitarian-Universalists, where I am fairly certain the members would vote "yes" they would save Jesus. Universalism, the theological belief that, ultimately, all souls will be reconciled with God, requires no such sacrifice. It is something to think about.

Pat Conroy, one of the great novelists of our time, focused on family dysfunction in *The Prince of Tides* and *The Great Santini* and on institutional cruelty in *The Water is Wide* and *The Lords of Discipline*. He turned his personal pain into a gentle, loving, caring, and productive life. The pricks and stabs of cruelty transformed into literature, and a rich, accomplished life grew in its place.

Another novelist whose early life was unfortunate was James Michener. Michener did not know his biological parents and was raised by an adoptive mother. His descriptions of his early life and abuse in orphanages and at the hands of church authorities are frightening to read. There is a story of a reporter saying to Michener, "You had a very tough childhood, some very bad experiences. Aren't you lucky that you can use this past experience as a writer?" Michener replied, "Yes, I suppose you are right. I do use that experience in my writings, but I would have had it the other way." (Another one of those asides: both Michener and Conroy were accomplished basketball players and attributed some of their survival to it.)

Isaac Lidsky played Weasel on NBC's *Saved by the Bell: The New Class* before losing his sight. He was the first blind person to serve as a law clerk for the U.S. Supreme Court. "Going blind taught me to live my life with eyes wide open. Blindness gave me a vision."

Some people tell us that grief is grief and that the pain of loss negotiates its way through our lives regardless of its source. Others might argue that some pain runs deeper than others, and even if the process is the same, the depth and duration affect us. I think it is a universal hope that we, as parents, will never see the death of our children. And yet, we also know that it can and does happen, and parents are left to grieve, to cope with the unbearable. Nothing cuts like the loss of a child. It is the death of the future. It steals our dreams and robs us of anticipated joy. I worked for many years with SHARE, a group developed to help parents of newborn infant death, miscarriage, and stillbirth. These parents lost their child, often before any loving touch or even a brief moment of life, or, perhaps, only minutes before the child was gone. Their grief was often physical and experienced as some have described as "Empty Arms," a physical experience of pain in the arms from not being able to hold a baby, an empty ache. What I learned from these parents was that they came to discover within themselves a capacity for pain they did not know they had and a strength to cope with the unbearable.

There is something of a trick in all this. Some people believe that it is hard times that develop hardy people. Maria

Sharapova has said, for example, "I don't know a lot of strong people who have had an easy past."

Ernest Hemingway said life can break us . . . some are strongest in their broken places. It would be a mistake to believe that hard times make us stronger. In Chinese, the word "Crisis" is said to be formed by two parts: Danger and Opportunity. It is not Hard Times alone that produces strong, hardy people but, rather, the successful resolution of those conflicts, events, situations, and tragedies of our lives that develop strength within us, and many have observed that the greatest strengths result in compassion. It is the strong who are kind, not the weak. The successful resolution of tragedies is that we get better, not bitter. We can learn in the struggle with the tragedies of our lives that our past is not our potential and that the future lies before us with the possibility that it is not the breaking that makes us strong but the healing. Robert Browning Hamilton has a lovely little poem titled "Along the Road" that teaches that sometimes, in life, our tragedies have lessons to teach.

Along the Road

I walked a mile with Pleasure...

But left me none the wiser...

I walked a mile with Sorrow...

...oh, the things I learned from her

When Sorrow walked with me.

We all make mistakes. Life comes with a full set of obstacles. We have to navigate from one stage of life to another and often have to relearn the lessons of the past. Sometimes there is a resolution, and sometimes there is not. Hard times can teach, and we know that even down to the muscles, it is overcoming the weight of life that strengthens. It is important to remember that it is not always necessary to lift the weight alone. That is one of the lessons of hard times. "A burden shared is a burden halved."

Some would have us believe that life must be made purposely hard so children will not grow up soft. A sort of parental "sink or swim," "survival of the fittest," or "only the strong survive" mentality. Those who believe that we have to make life hard on purpose so that children will become strong adults are wrong. There is no need to purposefully make life difficult. We know, those who have lived awhile, that life has tragedy enough without inserting unnecessary obstacles to toughen us up. There is a corresponding mistake of preventing children or people in general from facing the challenges of life. If we line the road with false success, then they do not have to develop their own true strength.

The Harry Potter Play - "Harry Potter and the Cursed Child" has an instructive passage. Harry is speaking to Dumbledore.

Harry: I need your help. I need your advice. ... Albus [Harry's son] is in danger. How do I protect my son, Dumbledore?

Dumbledore: You ask me, of all people, how to protect a boy in danger? We cannot protect the young from harm. The pain must and will come.

Harry: So I'm supposed to stand and watch?

Dumbledore: No. You're supposed to teach him how to meet life.

Sometimes, bravado, showmanship, posturing, or bullying pass for strength, but it is often revealed as false by a true life test. Once I was in Georgia, and a hurricane blew through the community where I was. We sheltered up for the night, and in the morning, when we came out, we discovered that some of the mighty oaks for which the community was well known had simply toppled during the wind. Huge, beautiful, tall, and magnificent trees had just blown over. One would think that in their majesty, they would withstand the onslaught of those winds, but no, they were blown over to reveal they were hollow on the inside. Mere shells. All appearance and no substance. Down in Texas, they say, "All Hat and No Horse." Often, it is trying times that show those with true substance. Those who have faced the wind before and developed the resilience to withstand the blast of circumstance.

The people truly worthy to be in your life are the ones who help you through hard times and stick with you after the hard times pass. Life gives us sufficient crises filled with danger and opportunity. Out of these crises, it is apparent that many of us develop a resilience to hard times that not only carries us through but strengthens us and sometimes, often, frequently leads to positive outcomes. Psychologists label this phenomenon the Hardiness Factor (See Chapter 5 for more on this). Hardiness is a combination of three attitudes: commitment (stick-to-a-tive-ness), control (I'm not a helpless victim of circumstance), and challenge (I have skills, talents, training, and education I can use) that together provide the courage and motivation needed to turn stressful circumstances from potential calamities into opportunities for personal growth and even situational change.

What are we to make of all of this? We should all look at the tragedies of life and say, "Thank You for my troubles. They have made me a better person." Of course not! Are you nuts? I haven't changed my name from Dave to Pollyanna. What we would hope for is a life with loving parents, firm and kind; gentle teachers; a partner, perhaps children who are happy and well-launched; opportunity in life as Freud phrased it, "Lieben und Arbeiten." Freud viewed love and work as equally essential elements of mental health and fulfillment. We can recognize that even the darkest of moments can be faced with a hopeful heart, if not for the crisis itself, at least for the growth it can evoke.

Bob Ross, remember Bob Ross, the artist, on Saturday morning television? He once said that he never made mistakes when painting. He only had "Happy Accidents." We do not know what life will bring us. We do know, as one of the gifts of aging, that hard times do come, unavoidably, and that preparation for that is the recognition that even the hard times can ultimately provide us with a richer, more meaningful life. We know from the lives of others that they have managed to survive and even prosper despite suffering some of life's hardest blows. Years ago, there was a physical barrier that all believed was impossible to overcome. Many had tried, and all failed. It was impossible, beyond human possibility. It was the 4-minute mile. Then, on May 6, 1954, Roger Bannister broke that barrier. He shattered it in 3 minutes 59.4 seconds. Impossible! Bannister's record lasted just 46 days. What one person can do, another can do.

If you cull history, you will find an amazing number of stories like the ones above. Humans have the capacity not only to survive hard times but to rebound and even profit from adversity.

There is a single word for this. It is Hope. Let me be clear here that I'm not talking about being an Optimist where I believe everything is going to turn out positive. (See Chapter 25 for more on this). Instead, I am talking about a hard reality where the truth, the hard truth, the demonstrable truth, is that the future is unknown. The word has not been written, the case isn't settled, the fat lady hasn't sung, and the last card hasn't been played. The future is open, and because it is open, I can hope.

Rose Kennedy, no stranger to human tragedy, once said, "Birds sing after storms. Why shouldn't people feel as free to delight in whatever sunlight remains to them?"

Oh, and one other word comes to mind. We can labor in the workshop of fulfillment and strive to succeed, and there is a magic potion for success. It is called sweat. So Freud. Listen up. Arbiten und Lieben und Schweiss. (Sweat!).

Thorns Have Roses

2
MIRACLES

Golden filtered trees stretch toward the sky
Reaching as if to touch the Sun
Silver flakes of snow drift toward the Earth
Mindlessly touching our senses
White water splashes from the mountains
Washing winter's cold touch from the land
Black earth breaks open
Turning fields from rest to plenty
Green grass of summer rushes from hill to hill
Causing us to pause in the hurry of life
to wonder
at
Miracles

Thorns Have Roses

3
PUT ME IN COACH

I saw a cartoon of two dinosaurs looking at Noah's Ark departing, and one said to the other, "Was that today?" (Forgive the dreadful mixing of geologic time periods, and I know dinosaurs and humans are separated by 65 million years, but it's still funny!) Plus, it got me thinking that some folks are like these Dinosaurs – life happens to them. Kind of like Weather Vanes, any way the wind blows there they go. Blown about by the shifting forces of society, the desires of others, and the whims of the powerful in their lives, wondering why the ship sailed without them.

Life demands that we take a chance. I'm hard-pressed to think of any life endeavor that does not involve risks. Boat trips involve risks. Relationships involve risks. Having children involves risks. Driving on the Interstate involves risks.

There is clearly a paradox in this risk business. We are all faced with decisions. We can live our lives on purpose and risk failure. We can renounce purpose and risk the dangers of happenstance. But, decisions risk success as well.

If you think about it, what is the opposite of purpose? It is aimlessness, negligence, avoidance, thoughtlessness, and carelessness. I'm not fond of mechanical metaphors to help explain human behavior, but one seems appropriate here. Ignore any piece of machinery, and it will break down eventually. Bicycle chains need oil. Automobile wheels need alignment. Coffee makers need cleaning. To avoid maintenance is to invite future repairs. It is true for human endeavors as well. We need to maintain ourselves. As we say down on the farm, sometimes in life, the fertilizer hits the windmill. Good doesn't just happen regularly; it is planned and maintained. When fertilizer happens, we can clean it up.

The Harvard Business School did a study years ago. The research from this study showed that students who set goals were the ones who had accomplished the most by the end of the study. While the study tied "accomplishment" to income, living a good life isn't mostly about money. Let me just say one word about money and move on. Clearly, poverty hurts people: physically, intellectually, emotionally, and socially. All these are affected by poverty. We know that money has a threshold value and to fall below that threshold invites a host of environmental, nutritional, physical, safety, medical, and social dangers that reduce the odds of a healthy and fulfilling life. One of the great indicators of human resilience, however, is even with the deck stacked against them, the children of poverty frequently emerge to lead full, meaningful lives. For someone like me, who grew up not dirt poor, but way down the socioeconomic ladder, education was the way out. With education came purpose, goals, and aspirations.

Just consider a question. Is it too much to ask that since we are endowed by nature with the capacity to seek from life what we want, can we not ask it? We aren't guaranteed to get what we want, of course. But that isn't the question. The question is "Are we capable?" and given the ordinary and expected tools of birth, the answer is "Yes, we are capable" and "Yes, we can ask."

Why is this important? Remember, it isn't guaranteed, and this gets a tiny bit complicated. Somewhere around the 1920s, Einstein proposed what is called the Theory of Relativity. Lots of folks think that the theory was so complex that only a few people in the world could understand it, but that wasn't true. Physicists all over the world immediately understood what Einstein proposed. It was a "Slap Your Forehead" moment in the history of physics. "Of course," they said, "That helps a lot." It not only changed physics, but it also changed science. It changed scientific thinking and drifted over into philosophy and then on into psychology and even weather forecasting, for example. Remember when we were kids, the weather would come on, and they would sing a little song- "Everybody talks about it. No one does a thing about it. About what? The Weather! Is it cold, is it hot, is it cloudy, rain, or snow? Here's the Weatherman, the guy who'll know." (All the weather forecasters were apparently male). Then, the weather forecaster would come on and say, with authority, "Tomorrow it's going to snow." Or, "It will be sunny tomorrow with a high of 87." We don't do that anymore. The weather is now based on probability. "There's an 80% chance of rain tomorrow." Or, they might say, "It would be wise to carry an umbrella tomorrow. I'm just saying. Chances are." Einstein did that. Life, the physical universe, and even weather forecasting doesn't come in black and white. It comes with probability.

Back to our theme. So you would like to get a new iPhone or a pickleball racket for your birthday. So you hope, and you wish upon a star, do pretty much a lot of hoping, and the one thing you don't do is tell your family that you would like to have a new pickleball racket. Then, you don't get one. Big Surprise. What you have done is put your family in the position of being mind readers. So, what are the probabilities that of the many possible gifts you might want, they are going to guess you want a pickleball racket? Let's just say you say, "I would love a pickleball racket for my birthday." Now, other things being equal, what are the odds of you getting a new racket? No guarantee, but the probability has certainly shifted in your favor.

Now, living with purpose is not concerned mainly with such trivial matters as wishing for gifts. It isn't concerned only with the peripheral but with the core aspects of life as well. I can plop two bucks down on a "quick pick" rather than carefully selecting my numbers because I'm not risking much, and the odds are the same anyway. But, selecting a partner for marriage is an entirely different proposition. We don't call up the agency and say, "I'm ready to get married. Send over anybody!" This one requires a little more consideration.

Living with purpose is a process of self-knowledge, realistic possibility, and, yes, risks. So, what constitutes a Purposeful Life? What might be guidelines or steps along the way? I read a little cynical complaint that read, "If the road of life is so well traveled, how come nobody knows the way?"

In fact, it is a well-traveled path. In truth there are lots of recommended ways to travel it, all of them worthy. The Ten Commandments, Lao Tzu, the Tao, The Four Noble Truths, The Eight Fold Path, the 12 Steps of AA, or Confucius (go on the internet and you will find 45 ways to live life to the fullest or 101 ways to live life with gusto). There is no shortage of good advice. Any one of them is worthy. If you followed them, you would be the better.

Which one is right? Ah, and there is the rub. Life comes to us in a variety of ways; it has many faces and many voices, and it may well be that one size does not fit all. So even with the great advice that is out there, it still comes down to you and me, and we have to decide.

Even with all that great advice out there, I'm going to go out on a limb and make some suggestions (with apologies to Jesus, Confucius, Lao Tzu, and the Buddha). Let's start with Goals. Some are big and lifelong. Some are immediate. Both are necessary. Here's the thing about goals. Here is some more research. Children with high self-esteem grow up in families/environments that have "reasonably high" expectations (goals) of them. Apparently, one "secret" to a fulfilling life is setting goals that are high and reasonable.

Two students of spiritual masters meet on a road, and one says to the other. "My master can walk across the water and point his finger at a rock on the far shore to carve out his name! What does your master do?" The second student replied, "My master eats when he is hungry and sleeps when he is tired." Living with purpose is a process of self-knowledge, realistic possibilities, and risks. Many young athletes might aspire to become professionals, but the odds are heavily stacked against them. There are about 1.1 million high school football players in the US, 70,000 college players, about 1700 professionals, with about 250 drafted each year. So, from 1.1 million to 1700. Not good odds. We should not discourage the dream but encourage a broad vision of the future. For the great majority of us, Education is a far better bet. So in this matter of self-knowledge, realistic possibility, and probability rest the foundation for goal setting. Denzel Washington reminds us that a dream without a plan is only a dream. If I could paraphrase Denzel Washington, I would also add that a plan without action is only a plan. So it becomes necessary not only to Dream but to Plan and not only to Plan but to Act.

That brings us to another purposeful life skill. Purposeful living is a process of moving Assertively in the direction of our goals. *Assertiveness* is one of those tricky words. One of my teachers once said that "anytime someone makes an argument in an either/or fashion, then you can be pretty sure both of them are wrong." So, we are often offered the choice of being passive or being aggressive.

Assertiveness is the third alternative. We can't live purposefully if we passively follow the dictates of family, society, or culture or give up our goals and dreams because of family, social, or peer pressure. To live purposefully isn't the path of least resistance or to give up because it is hard, and it isn't to bully or diminish others or to use them aggressively for our own ends. It is a process of setting reasonable goals for ourselves and actively seeking a way forward. Assertiveness means having a realistic understanding of the possibilities of success and moving consistently in that direction.

Purpose carries *Responsibility*. "Doing your own thing" is a fine philosophy so long as you live in a society of one. Hermits notwithstanding, no one does. Some people insist on the myth of the Self-Made Success, but such a person does not exist. We all have help along the way. Here's the truth. We would not have made it without the help of many. Here is one more thing to remember in your shyness to seek help. To receive help isn't a shame; it is an honor. Help is offered and help comes from people who want to help because they care for you and want you to succeed. It might be worth thinking that those who insist that you do it alone are, perhaps, not as interested in your success as they are in their own philosophy. So accept help when you need it, and do not accept help when you do not. That is responsible action. Therefore, our behavior is limited by respect for the goals and purposes of others. Responsibility means that as we move in the direction of our dreams, we do so with regard for others. Responsibility requires that the means be worthy of the end, and demanding responsible action from ourselves is the preventive for selfishness.

Living with purpose isn't wishful thinking. Our lives truly are not at the mercy of a twinkling star. We can learn, develop, and practice the skills we need to move toward our goals. This is called *Competence*. Here's another research finding. People who are good at something think better of themselves. It doesn't so much matter what it is. It is just that they are good at it, and that covers a lot of other doubts. Some Native American cultures practiced this in their naming of people. Someone might be called "Wooden Leg," which meant they could walk all day. A prophet might be named "Stands on the Mountain." In the Kevin Costner movie **Dances with Wolves**, the title character is named "Dances with Wolves" because of his relationship with a wolf and "Stands with a Fist" is a determined and angry woman. When asked, as a young man, why he read so much, Abraham Lincoln is supposed to have replied, "I am studying now so that when my time comes, I will be ready." It is sound advice. Luck happens when opportunity meets preparation. Dreams require preparation.

If we are to move consistently in the direction of our goals, we need *Commitment and Perseverance*. Some goals are small and temporary. They come easily and with little effort. Some are considerable and demand sacrifice and effort. Confucius reminds us, "It does not matter how slowly you go so long as you do not stop." Some dreams require perspiration, yet because it is our dream, we find the resolve, the time, and the strength to pursue it.

Resilience is the ability to bounce back from disappointments, and it separates the fulfilled person from the discouraged, undernourished one. Another name for this quality is the Hardiness Factor (See Chapter 5 for more on The Hardiness Factor). Life has risks. Risks can bring failure.

Failure brings challenges and the will to face challenges – to do it again, if necessary. Joe Louis is supposed to have said, "Getting knocked down isn't important. It's getting up that's important."

A purposeful life is characterized by *Creativity*. Even the most ordinary goals of life are sometimes not responsive to standard solutions. When something doesn't work and your solution is doing the same thing over and over and expecting a different result is the definition of insanity. Life is a process of flexibility and change. The creative life is one of imagination, fantasy, whimsy, resourcefulness, and ingenuity. To be creative means that, attitudinally, we never run out of alternatives. In fact, creatively approaching our goals may change the very goal itself and transform it into another goal that is equally or even more satisfying. Serendipity plays a role in living, and flexibility permits us to profit from it. Creativity is the ability to turn chance into purpose.

A Nobel Prize winner entered his field because his girlfriend gave him a physics book. She bought it because it was on sale at the bookstore. That's life! The good in good fortune comes from our recognition of its usefulness in our lives, while the rigid pursuit of goals, the driven preoccupation with a single end, is not purposeful living. Purposeful living demands that we improvise, alter, and adapt to changing situations and events. Obsession is blind save to its passion. Purposeful living is open, flexible, and adaptive!

We are an odd species, and given the nature of the world, we really don't have much business being here at all. Other creatures are stronger, faster, and have better senses of sight and smell. Save for three things: one is the opposable thumb, the second is language, and the third is our ability to cooperate, all fueled by our unique brain. As individuals, we don't have much of a chance in the world. We are born incapable of survival, except we are cared for in a very long childhood. We are bound to each other. Each of us is interdependent and connected to the interdependent web of all existence of which we are a part. Turn on any water tap, flip on a light switch, and at the end of a continuous chain of interdependence stands an unknown ally.

Involvement with People is an aspect of purposeful living. Much is made of our alienation from one another in modern society, and I do not wish to dispute that we could be kinder and more caring toward one another. Still, it is wrong to assume that ours is an uncaring society. We see acts of courage and humanity in every disaster. An earthquake in San Francisco collapses a bridge on an interstate highway that cuts through the ghetto. In the rubble, the residents of the ghetto climb out from their modest homes to help the accountants, attorneys, and business people with whom they share little in common except their common humanity in a crisis. Strangers risk their lives to bring down a stranded mountain climber. Firefighters rush into burning homes, and although it might be their job, there is also a belief in and a commitment to compassion, altruism, and service to humanity. Muhammad Ali said, "Service is the rent we pay for our place on earth." Whatever solitary path we walk, we do not walk it without support. There is a difference between being alone and being lonely. When we are involved with people, our tasks may be solitary and exclusive, but we need not be lonely.

What we desire for ourselves, we must permit to others. This is the foundation of social justice. It is also a necessary part of purposeful living. It might be called a *Democratic Character Structure*. Look at the picture below. This is the President of the United States. Some call the President the most powerful person in the world. And it is a fist bump with a custodian!

President Barack Obama fist-bumps custodian Lawrence Lipscomb in the Eisenhower Executive Office Building.

I put an exclamation point at the end of the last sentence because I want to emphasize the barrier it shattered. It's a way of being in a world that believes in the acceptance of all people regardless of class, education, ethnic differences, and the like. They don't act superior toward anyone.

Juxtapose this with the President of a corporation looking out the window at the grounds crew cutting grass and turning to a group and saying, "I love to watch the little people work." What dream is worth the dehumanization, exploitation, and ruin of another? I heard Barbara Bush, the former First Lady, give a commencement speech in which she reminded the graduates that the goals we pursue must be chosen with care. She nudged us with the thought that at life's end, we don't plague ourselves with musing about how better life would have been if we had just spent a little more time at the office, made one more sale, or driven a Cadillac instead of a Lexus. What we review is whether we did right by our children, whether our decisions unnecessarily hurt others, and whether we were of some use in the world. We contribute little to raising healthy children, consistently deciding in favor of people, or contributing much to the world if we do not respect people. Our human history is teeming with scoundrels and zealots, lunatics, and monsters whose contribution to humanity has been damaged lives, ravaged communities, and dysfunctional societies that responsible and caring people have had to spend their lives repairing. Democratic Character Structure permits us to move in the direction of our dreams as we give to others what we want for ourselves.

What is the outcome of living with purpose? It is meaning. Meaning doesn't come with birth. It isn't apparent in the workings of the Universe. There is seemingly no particular meaning in the physical universe. The earth spins; it rotates around the sun; the tides ebb and flow, but the universe is apparently doing nothing and going nowhere in particular.

Purpose comes through experience, knowledge, and the choices and decisions we make in life. There is great latitude in living, and while it is obvious that some have greater sovereignty than others, many of us can have a voice in deciding our path. It is likely that by the decisions we make and the dreams we pursue, we create our worth in the world. I do not mean worth to others. I mean worth to ourselves. I mean an Internal Life Review that concludes, "My life is worthwhile; the costs are not too high; the fare is not too steep; it is worth the trip."

4
THE COURAGE TO BE IMPERFECT

We all know the fable of Little Red Riding Hood. She went to Grandma's house where the Big Bad Wolf had eaten Grandma and dressed up like Grandma, tricked Little Red Riding Hood. "What big teeth you have Grandma." "All the better to eat you with!" Well, the story doesn't end well. But many of us don't know the story of Little Blue Riding Hood. Little Blue Riding Hood was going to meet her Grandmother for the first time. She didn't know exactly where Grandma lived. She came to a fork in the road and it was a twisting wooded path, and she could not see very far down the lane. She decided to take the right-hand path. She soon came upon a little village, and the first person she met was a boy named Jack. She met the friendly Butcher, the Baker, and Candlestick Maker. She met the woodcutter. They told her where Grandma lived, so she started through the woods to Grandma's house. But then the Big Bad Wolf jumped out to grab her, and she yelled out for help. Jack got there first because he was nimble. The Woodcutter and the Butcher got there next. The Big Bad Wolf was frightened off. Little Blue Riding Hood ran to Grandma's house, where she was safe. Grandma, Little Blue Riding Hood, Jack, the Woodcutter, the Butcher, and all the people who lived in the little Village became close friends over the years, and the Wolf didn't come around much anymore because he knew that if he tried to grab Little Blue Riding Hood or Grandma or anyone from that little Village that everyone would come to help and he would be in big trouble.

Little Blue Riding Hood grew up and went to college, and when Grandma passed away peacefully, she inherited the house in the forest. She married Jack, and they established a software consulting business, and they lived happily ever after. Now, this happy story all happened because Little Blue Riding Hood made a mistake. She took the wrong path through the woods. She met people she would not have ordinarily met and made friends, and those friends became a part of her life and a part of her future happiness.

So, a question comes up. Why do we beat ourselves up when we foul up? We cuss. We say nasty things. We throw stuff. We hit things. It isn't a pretty sight! Why are we so concerned or even afraid of making mistakes? Well, being a bit mischievous and cynical here, but it all may have started with Freud and his structure of the personality. Freud proposed that we are made up of the Id, Ego, and Super Ego or, in German, Uber Ich (the Over I). The Super Ego is what might loosely be labeled a "conscience" or that nagging little voice we hear when we make a mistake or violate a rule. The Super Ego can grow very strong in some people. It may become a harping, carping, criticizing, and even punishing part of a person. So, to shut the Super Ego up, we toe the line, follow the rules, and plan carefully so that we don't hear the voice and experience GUILT.

So let's take a step back here - What is a mistake anyway? What is acceptable, and what is beautiful?

Beauty?

Sometimes, I think about a garden

with splendid soil and sunlight bright

with refreshing rain and careful hand

and look upon the rose that grows

full, rich, and fragrant.

And see the ribbon upon the vase

a prize justly won.

Sometimes, I see a gnarled tree

struggling to sink its roots

to find the sun from under the rock

to suck some nurture from the stingy soil

to drink a small taste from moistened ground

and look upon the tree that grows

bent, barely green, and dry

And see no ribbon

Yet I wonder what the Great Gardner would value more?

~David Welch

Why is it a mistake? It is a mistake because some Authority says so. Now, an Authority may range from a cruel dictator to the dictionary, but it is someone or something with power, and that power may range from the gallows to a "tsk-tsk." Now, here's an interesting thing: the more Democratized we become, the fewer mistakes we make. Why is that? In a Democracy, authority is shared.

Not all mistakes are alike, of course. A rough list of mistakes might include Catastrophic, Tough, and Meaningless. Catastrophic mistakes could be life and death and have no second chances. Tough mistakes are like Little Blue Riding Hood. There can be consequences, but the outcome can be readdressed. Finally, some mistakes are simply Meaningless – or, as they say in sports - "No harm; no foul." You forget to dot the "i," and the consequences are small, if any.

What do we do in the face of these mistakes? This chapter isn't about Catastrophic mistakes, and such mistakes lie beyond the scope of this chapter. Tough and Meaningless mistakes for which we unnecessarily punish ourselves are what we are dealing with.

Little Blue Riding Hood made a mistake and took the wrong path. The consequence was that she met new people, and ultimately, they saved her and Grandma. So mistakes can have positive as well as negative outcomes. Here's Thomas Edison on mistakes:

"I have not failed. I've just found 10,000 ways that won't work."

"I never view mistakes as failures – simply opportunities to find out what doesn't work."

"I've never made a mistake. I've only learned from experience."

Edison had transcended conventional wisdom and, rather than beat himself up for making a mistake, turned it to his advantage and used the information he gained from the mistake to try a better solution in the next experiment. I suspect that if you interviewed any research scientist, you would discover that most of their experiments result in "failure." Maya Angelou had some wisdom to share about letting go of mistakes. "If we all hold on to the mistake, we can't see our own glory in the mirror because we have the mistake between our faces and the mirror; we can't see what we're capable of being. You can ask forgiveness of others, but in the end, the real forgiveness is in one's own self."

Many years ago, a British physician and researcher had an unusual hobby. Using a petri dish and bacteria, he created images and designs that were astoundingly both creative and beautiful. He would dab the petri dish with bacteria and then place the dish in a cool cabinet overnight. He would examine them the next morning to see how his design had turned. He decided to change his procedure a bit, and after dabbing the dish with bacteria, he didn't place it in the cooler. Instead, he left it out on the counter. He returned about two weeks later to see the results and discovered mold in the dish. Under the microscope, he observed that the bacteria had died wherever the mold had grown. Alexander Fleming was awarded a Nobel Prize in Medicine for his discovery of Penicillin all stemming from an art project gone awry.

I mentioned Bob Ross a bit earlier, the Television painter who demonstrated his painting technique to us on the screen and in seminars. He once said he never made mistakes when painting. He only had "Happy Accidents." I am a painter. I hesitate to call myself an "Artist," but I have learned from Bob Ross. Sometimes, I start with an idea and can't seem to get it from my brain through the brush onto the canvas. I have had "Happy Accidents." I step back and simply begin again. I am Edison, Ross, and Little Blue Riding Hood.

So, in this business of mistakes, we need to do some rethinking, what psychologists call "Reframing." We need to redefine "perfection." Let's go to baseball again as an example. Pardon me for using sports metaphors. I'm an American male – what can I say? Now, back to baseball. It's the bottom of the 9th inning. The score is tied. There is a runner on third, and there are two outs. If we score, we win the game. The batter has a count of 3 and 2. Now, for the home team, a perfect outcome would be a home run over the fence. Or is it. Might not it also be a "Texas Leaguer" that drops into shallow center field or a "Seeing Eye" grounder that winds its way through the infield as the runner scores from 3rd? The game is won. No better outcome (for the Home Team) is possible. We might redefine "Perfection" as the best possible outcome.

Sometimes, a mistake is just a mistake. A long time ago, our son, then nine years old, played soccer in the city league. He was a goalkeeper. Half in jest and half in earnest, his coach called him "Wonder Goalie." Once, in one of those games, a ball rolled slowly toward the goal, and he went to pick it up, and it rolled through his legs and into the goal. I was crushed and knew he would be inconsolable. I prepared myself as a Dad to be ready to comfort him as he came to the sidelines at the end of the game. He came over, and I said something like, "That was a tough one." He said, "Sometimes I make a mistake." Nine years old! Instructing his father on how to handle failure and emotions! Nine years old! Sometimes a mistake is just a mistake. Let it go and move on.

Some years ago, a British physician coined the term "Good Enough Mother" to make the point that parents don't have to be "perfect" to raise healthy and decent children into adulthood. They simply have to be "good enough," and then the child has the platform from which to launch into adulthood.

Some advice comes from a wise but unknown Roman philosopher who said, "Non Sudare Parva Vasa." This means, roughly translated into English, something like - "Don't Sweat the Small Stuff." Then, as modified in America, "and remember it's all small stuff."

When I was a boy growing up in Tennessee, baseball was the sport we played. We played from morning to night wherever and whenever we could. I could even play it by myself. I could practice pitching and fielding by throwing the baseball against the front steps of our house. If you threw the ball just right, you could make the return a grounder or a fly ball and get in your infield practice. I could practice hitting by throwing the ball up in the air, and as it came down hit away. (There was the shortcoming of having to retrieve the ball after you hit it.) I imagined playing in a game and throwing the ball at the steps, fielding it, and pretending to throw the runner out at first base. I could throw the ball up and smack in the game-winning run. That memory was revived in all its sweetness when I first heard the song "The

Greatest" sung by Kenny Rogers (written by Don Schlitz). It is the story of a little boy, just like me, standing in a field and throwing up the ball to hit. He imagines himself to be "the greatest player of them all." So, in the song, he throws up a ball, swings, and misses. He is undeterred. He throws up the ball again, swings, and misses again. Well, that's strike two. He doesn't make any excuses but stares at his bat, settles down, digs in, and thinks to himself, "I'm the greatest when the game is on the line." So he throws the ball in the air, swings with all his might, and the ball falls to the ground. That's strike three! He picks up his ball, puts his bat on his shoulder, and walks toward home. He thinks to himself, "I am the greatest; that is a fact, but even I didn't know I could pitch like that."

What can we do with the inevitable mistakes of life? When the ball falls to the ground. There is a poem, Desiderata, by Max Ehrmann that has these lines of wisdom. "Beyond a Wholesome Discipline, Be Gentle with Yourself."

So it is with the tough and meaningless mistakes in our lives.

Thorns Have Roses

5
THE HARDINESS FACTOR: HOW THE TOUGH GET GOING WHEN THE GOING GETS TOUGH

It isn't a secret that we have been through some tough times. The Pandemic of 2020 frightened, frustrated, and stressed us all even as it continues. We were worried about our loved ones as well as ourselves. When could we get a shot, and how effective would it be? We were stuck at home (no pun intended!) and exhausted our creative energies to stay on track. What to do? Well, luckily, there is the field of Psychology to come to the rescue. It turns out that psychologists have studied this business of how people can cope with stress in their lives and have even identified some characteristics of people who seem to do okay even in stressful times. They call it "The Hardiness Factor." We will take a look at those characteristics and even make a suggestion or two on how to tough it out!

Commitment

"Once there was a silly old ram" is a line from a song written by Sammy Cahn years ago. That "silly old ram" had it in its head that it would butt a hole in a dam. No one could convince it that a ram couldn't do any such thing. The ram didn't quit. He kept ramming that dam. Well, KERPLUNK, there goes the dam! The song was entitled "High Hopes," and that's what the ram had . . . high hopes. Now, that silly little song sung by Frank Sinatra named "High Hopes" actually captures an important psychological principle, namely Commitment. One of the three characteristics of Psychological Hardiness. The other two are Control and Challenges. The Three Cs of Hardiness. Let's talk about commitment. You know the story of the two frogs that fell into a bucket of milk? Two frogs were just merrily hopping along one day and accidentally fell into a bucket of milk. The sides were so steep they couldn't climb out. One of the frogs just didn't see any way to escape, gave up, and sank to the bottom. The other frog didn't see any way out either but kept on trying. It kept on struggling. It kept on kicking. But then, the frog began to feel something firm below its legs. Its constant churning had turned the milk into butter. From the now-hardened surface of the butter, the frog jumped out of the bucket. The point, of course, is that dealing with stuff in life takes more than one attempt. Interestingly, everything that makes our daily living easier, more productive, more enjoyable, and more pleasurable now was created because of a problem in the past. So it is obvious that the problems of the day can overwhelm us. They can wash over us like a rising tide and seem irresistible. Here's a fact: the rising water can drown us all. So why do some endure and survive, and others sink? That's the thing. It isn't so much the problems we have to face as it is the psychological way in which we solve them. In Hamlet, Shakespeare gave us this, "There is nothing either good or bad, but thinking makes it so." It turns out that activities, things, and other people all are a buffer against being overwhelmed. Research revealed that people who coped with stress best had a tendency to involve themselves in activities and were interested in and curious about how others were coping and dealing with their problems. Two quick ideas come immediately to mind: First, Social and Civic Clubs, churches and other community organizations and the Internet. We have been good about reaching out to others, Zooming with classes and interaction. Second, the internet allows us to reach beyond our community for ideas and even for entertainment. I'm a poker player. I play poker every day. I'm also cheap. So I play for free. I also play chess. And checkers. And do crosswords. And read. And make hiking sticks. And paint. I also have a partner who makes long lists of things for me to do! Let's finish this section with a definitional quote. People with the Hardiness Factor "do not believe in giving up no matter what kind of obstacle they face; they seem to believe in the purpose of life and also the bond with the people they care about."

Control

I've written about the Serenity Prayer in other chapters. One popular version of the prayer goes like this.

God grant me the Serenity to accept the things I cannot change

The Courage to change the things I can

and the wisdom to know the difference.

Much of the focus of this prayer has been on the first line. Serenity and the power of God are a focus and a conviction that one should "Let Go and Let God." I'm not going to argue with that, but for me, it is the second line that is the most powerful. It clearly says that some things lie within our control. This factor is the tendency of hardy people to believe and act as if they can influence the events surrounding them through their own actions. There is the story of three baseball umpires discussing their role behind the plate. One says, "Some of 'em is balls, and some of 'em is strikes. I call 'em like they is." The second says, "Some's balls and some's strikes, and I call 'em like I see 'em." The third says, "Some's balls and some's strikes, but they ain't nothin' till I call 'em."

There's the clue. If we go back to the Serenity Prayer again, it also teaches that part of our control is about sorting out those things over which we can have an influence and those which we cannot. Abraham Maslow, an American psychologist, had a funny way of saying this. "Find out what you are not good at and don't do it." So the flip side of the coin is to do what you are good at, and that brings control into your life. Back when I was in the working world, I had a habit. One of the first things I did in the morning at work was sit down and make a list of my obligations for the day. Then, I would prioritize it. My rule was to do the hard stuff first. When I had to push stuff off to another day, it was usually the easy, less important things on my list. I felt good about my day's accomplishments and in control. Let me give you an ancient parable from the Far East. There is the parable of the arrows that comes from the Buddha. The parable of the second arrow is a well-known Buddhist story about dealing with suffering more skillfully. It is said the Buddha once asked a student, 'If a person is struck by an arrow, is it painful? If the person is struck by a second arrow, is it even more painful?' He then went on to explain, 'In life, we can't always control the first arrow. The first arrow causes us physical pain, which we can't ignore. The second arrow is the mental pain and suffering we add on top of the physical pain. This is the pain we can control." This is sometimes interpreted as meaning that pain is inevitable, but suffering is optional. I'm not sure I would go that far. To my mind, there are clearly situations where to experience suffering and grief is the human and loving response. However, it is true that our interpretation of events plays a large role in how we experience them and that we can over-dramatize what happens to us. Sometimes, we look at our problems through Binoculars.

Challenge

Challenge is the belief that change is the natural order of life, rather than stability, and instead of threatening our security, it provides the a motivating chance for personal growth. John F. Kennedy made the following phrase famous in his campaigns in 1959 and 1960: In the Chinese language, the word "crisis" is composed of two characters, one representing danger and the other, opportunity. Some argue that Kennedy misunderstood the Chinese character, but, as we learn from John Wayne's movie "Who Shot Liberty Valence," when the legend becomes fact, print the legend. Let's take it at face value. Crises can be dangerous, and yet they also offer the opportunity to find strengths and talents within ourselves that had not been called into use before. Hardy people seem to accept hard times as the normal course of events that being alive brings with it. They see it more as an opportunity than as a threat. How do they do that? There's another psychological concept you may have heard of. It is labeled "reframing." Another name is a Defense Mechanism or Defensive Construct. Aesop gave us a famous one, Sour Grapes. The fox wanted the grapes, but they hung too high on the vine. After jumping, climbing, and clawing without being able to reach them, the fox finally gave up and muttered, "I bet they were sour anyway!" Who would want sour grapes? So it's not worth the effort. It is possible to see these hard times as ones in which we can find a better version of ourselves. A version that sees the struggles, isolation, and stress as paths to greater creativity and challenge. Let's end on a light but thoroughly uplifting note where hard times didn't win, but Reframing did.

The Greatest

Little boy in a baseball hat,

Stands in a field, with his ball and bat, . . .

Swings his bat, with all his might, . . .

and the baseball falls, and that's strike three.

Now it's supper time, and his Mama calls,

little boy starts home with his bat and ball,

says "I am the greatest, that is a fact,

but even I didn't know, I could pitch like that.

("The Greatest" by Don Schlitz and sung by Kenny Rogers)

A little boy with a bat, through the power of imagination, can transform himself from a batter into a pitcher and change failure into success. We can transform a pandemic and fear into commitment, courage, and challenge and transform stress and social isolation into action, involvement, and a sense of control in one's life.

We are the greatest and that's a fact. But even we didn't know we could adapt like that.

Thorns Have Roses

6
THE GOLDILOCKS ZONE, THE INVERTED "U" AND THE SECRET TO CONTENTMENT

I noticed a little piece on Holmes and Watson, two of my favorite characters from fiction. It seems Sherlock Holmes and Dr. Watson go on a camping trip. After a good dinner and a bottle of wine, they set up their tent and retired for the night to go to sleep. Some hours later, Holmes wakes up and nudges his faithful friend. "Watson, look up at the sky and tell me what you see." "I see millions and millions of stars, Holmes," replies Watson. "And what do you deduce from that?" Watson ponders for a minute. "Well, astronomically, it tells me that there are millions of galaxies and potentially billions of planets. I can see that God is all-powerful, and that we are a small and insignificant part of the universe. What does it tell you, Holmes?" Holmes is silent for a moment. "Watson, my old friend," he says. "I deduce that someone has stolen our tent!"

Once upon a time, all good stories begin this way. Once upon a time, there was a little girl named Goldilocks. She went for a walk in the forest. Pretty soon, she came upon a house. She knocked, and when no one answered, she walked right in. At the table in the kitchen, there were three bowls of porridge. Goldilocks was hungry. She tasted the porridge from the first bowl. "This porridge is too hot!" she exclaimed.

So, she tasted the porridge from the second bowl. "This porridge is too cold," she said.

So, she tasted the last bowl of porridge. "Ahhh, this porridge is just right," she said happily, and she ate it all up.

Now I'm going to tell you another story. You might not have heard this one. Once upon a time, deep within the icy reaches of interstellar space, hidden in the vast, black emptiness of the universe, almost unnoticeable to the eye, there exists a tiny pebble of rock. One has to come very close before this speck gleams from the reflected light of a distant star and reveals itself as a blue-white marble suspended in space. Draw closer, and you will see that this strange little rock bustles with life, and against all understanding in the infinite, dark, cold, and void, it hangs there.

There is no apparent reason for the rock. It is simply there. The life that lives there lives there because the rock is there, not just anywhere but precisely where it is. A space traveler will tell you that traveling in space is a lonely venture, and indeed, one could sail for lifetimes without encountering anything at all. Perhaps, one would see a light, and it might be a star, but we would be disintegrated if we tried to draw near. If you chanced upon some rock, not a star, then it would be nothing more than a rock, as cold, dark, and desolate as space itself. But, this little rock, this little blue-white marble, is different. It is different because of where it is in space. It occupies what can only be called a magical place. It exists in the Goldilocks Zone. Like Goldilocks' porridge, it is just right. And the strangest thing of all on this strange little rock is... us.

Now, I'm going to tell you a third story. I'm pretty certain it is one you have not heard before, since, in truth, it has only begun to be told in the last 50 years or so. Now, we all know we are here because of this astrophysical phenomenon known as the Goldilocks Zone. In truth, we are here because of another astrophysical event as well. Physicists tell us that the Earth, for that is what this little rock came to be called, was formed in a gigantic universal gathering of matter four and a half billion (with a "b") years ago. As the Earth evolved, it has endured a number of catastrophic events, such as massive volcanic eruptions and gigantic asteroid strikes. Different life forms have appeared and disappeared through the years. One of the most successful creatures to evolve on Earth was the dinosaur. It dates back to 240 million years ago and dominated the Earth until about 65 million years ago. Then, one of those catastrophic events I just talked about happened. A massive asteroid struck the Earth. The asteroid, which had a diameter of about six miles, struck the Yucatan Peninsula and left a crater measuring 12 miles deep by 124 miles wide. The collision wiped out about 80 percent of the Earth's species alive on Earth at the time. The dinosaurs, unfortunately, did not survive. After 170 million years, the dinosaur was literally blasted into oblivion.

Why am I telling you this story of the demise of dinosaurs? Because that event allowed tiny mammals to emerge from the domination of the dinosaurs and begin the long evolutionary journey that eventually became us. That long process resulted in the genus Homo, a particular form of primate that began to dominate the African landscape. Around 200,000 years ago, at least three of these began to leave Africa and populate around the world. Homo Neanderthalus, Homo Erectus, and Homo Sapiens spread around the world and perhaps intermingled. Everything was going well until, yep, you guessed it, another catastrophic event. There have been an estimated five (5) of these in geological history. This time, a volcanic eruption, Mount Toba, spewed volcanic gases, lava, and ash, approximating 12,000 times the eruption of Mount St. Helens, covering the Earth and lasting from 6 to 10 years, with a corresponding 1000-year cold.

It caused the near extinction of the genus Homo Sapiens with only a few thousand Homo Sapiens surviving in East Africa (More about this in Chapter 18, The Story of Us). Yes, you heard me right. Out of the total population of homo sapiens living 70,000 years ago, only a few thousand, maybe as few as 10,000, survived this devastating climatic event. They survived in little bands of 20 or perhaps 100 individuals. They survived and prospered. Then, about 60,000 years ago, in a not fully understood evolutionary event, the human brain expanded. It is from those 10,000 survivors that we all count our history. What are we to make of all this? So here we are, something of a lucky happenstance in the universe with a big old brain that puzzles us constantly with wishes, hopes, dazzling possibilities, and sometimes troubling imaginings and hurtful negative self-condemnation.

What to do? What to do?

One thing is to figure out how to find enjoyment, happiness, and contentment in this gift of life we have inherited. Turns out that over the years, humans have actually figured out, to some degree, how to do that.

Let me just say a little bit about happiness. Happiness is one of those emotional states that might not be a reasonable goal to pursue. I know this seems a bit counterintuitive in our world since so many folks wish to be happy. It is one of the more frequently hoped-for states of being. Here's the rub: happiness is a fleeting emotion born out of some event or situation that is temporary. It isn't a lasting state of being. Enjoyment and contentment might, however, be more stable. As it happens, we do know something about enjoyment, contentment, and even happiness that is helpful. It is the Inverted "U" - a "U" looks like this (use the hand to make a "U"); the inverted "U" looks like this (use hand to make an upside-down "U") or something like a mound. Here's a secret: This Inverted "U" thing is a secret to a lot of life's problems. It goes like this. It is a graph with the amount or frequency along the bottom and enjoyment, contentment, or even healthiness along the side like this (Make the hand into an "L" shape). Down in the left corner, you have Zero amount and Zero contentment. Then as you move along the bottom to the right, you increase the amount, and there is a corresponding movement upward in contentment.

Now, let's take something pretty straightforward like food. On the left is starvation and ill health. As you add food, you become healthier and more satisfied. As you add more food, you become healthier and more satisfied until you reach a point where you do not need any more food; you are at your optimal weight and satisfaction. If you continue to eat, you add weight, health issues can increase, and satisfaction goes down. Until on the far right, you have morbid obesity and high personal dissatisfaction.

It works like this for alcohol, golf, sex, work, gardening, running, cooking, auto mechanics, skydiving, exercise, watering plants, or sunbathing. In fact, it seems to be the secret of life. Enjoyment, happiness, and contentment lie within a range. It is a secret many people and even many great religions have discovered. So many religions use the circle as a sacred symbol, advising balance as the secret of serenity. Philosophers have long advised us to use moderation; told us to be wary of the dangers of diminishing returns; not to put all our eggs in one basket; and to diversify our portfolio. Think about it. The Inverted "U" is the secret of life.

Let's cut to the chase. What does it take to be content with our lives? Again, it comes as a surprise that we know something about this too. It has to do with expectations. We live in a culture where we may have been misled all our lives. We have been taught since the crib to shoot for the stars; you can do anything; just do it, aim high, and dream big; the world is your oyster, you have to be dedicated to a single goal, second sucks. Another study has been conducted of on "High Achievers" and how driven they are. Yet, how often have the rest of us stopped and examined what is being measured in these studies and what is not? More often than not, it is money, and if not money, then celebrity, and if not celebrity, then status. Money, celebrity, and status are the measures of contentment in life in these studies of "High Achievers." I actually suspect not. I'm a representative of a particular class of people... old people. Let's do a poll of old people. I suspect that money (given the Inverted "U" thing), celebrity, and status would not rate high on the scale of contentment. I'd put my money on family, friends, health, and time as the real markers of success in life. I'll interject a note of caution. I am speaking from the perspective of years... many of them. Perhaps, drive has more importance earlier in life. Still, don't forget the Inverted "U."

As for contentment, the secret formula for that, at least as I read it in Reader's Digest, is to lower your expectations. Yes, rather than the driven Type "A" recommendations we have learned in the past, it seems the road to life contentment, enjoyment, and happiness is to appreciate what we have, want what we have, and be grateful for what we have. Drive a Buick rather than a Cadillac or a Chevy rather than a Buick... it's the same car anyway. We really don't need all the stuff we have right now. Maybe we don't need any more. I just read an unsettling article that said to get rid of our stuff right now. Our children don't want it! So testifies all the estate sales we go to every week. So now you know. Enjoyment, contentment, and happiness lie within a range, and more—more often than not—leads to discontent. It is the gentle way that leads to contentment. At least in my time of life. The secret to contentment . . . lower your expectations and be grateful for what you have.

7
PRAY TO GOD AND CONTINUE TO SWIM TOWARD SHORE

We face hard times in this world, and folks struggle with ways to cope. The title of this chapter, "Pray to God and Continue to Swim Toward Shore," sets some boundaries on how we approach the troubles of life. I am a part of another group of people who struggle with one of the hard realities of life, Al-Anon. Al-Anon is an organization for the families and friends of alcoholics. Al-Anon has but one purpose, which is to help families of alcoholics. I come from a family of alcoholics. Both my father and my brother were alcoholics and died of the disease. My brother's death certificate listed his cause of death as "alcoholism." It is the only death certificate I have seen that is so specific in its cause and reveals the ravages of that disease for him. Al-Anon, like Alcoholics Anonymous, follows the 12-step program. The first three steps of the program are:

1. We admitted we were powerless over alcohol – that our lives had become unmanageable.

2. Came to believe that a Power greater than ourselves could restore us to sanity.

3. Made a decision to turn our will and our lives over to the care of God as we understood him.

Those steps are often summarized as "I can't; He can: I'll let him." Or, the guidance many follow is to "Let Go and Let God." That is the first part of the title of this chapter, "Pray to God..."

But, there is more to Al-Anon's teaching. There is also the Serenity Prayer. Written by Reinhold Niebuhr, an American theologian, it is most often read as:

God Grant me the Serenity to accept the things I cannot change

the Courage to change the things I can

and the Wisdom to know the difference.

There is a continuing verse not often read:

Living one day at a time. Enjoying one moment at a time. Accepting hardship as the pathway to peace. Taking, as He did, this sinful world as it is, Not as I would have it. Trusting that He will make all things right if I surrender to His will. That I may be reasonably happy in this life, and supremely happy with Him forever in the next.

It is in the Serenity Prayer that the second part of the title of this reflection comes to life, "the courage to change the things I can." So we are told that there is a difference between those problems that lie outside our control and those over which we exercise some control.

There is a scene in the movie "Ben Hur" where Ben Hur returns to his childhood home after slavery in Rome to discover his father crippled and aided by a mute servant. The servant carries the old man on his shoulders, and the father says to Ben Hur, "Mallet without a tongue and I without life in my legs. Since then, I have been his tongue and he has been my legs. Together, we make a considerable man." The father cannot change his damaged legs, and the servant cannot speak, but they can manipulate their environment to turn it as best they can to their use.

There is the story of a man trapped by a hurricane. The rains are pouring down, and his neighbors came by in a small boat and said, "Jump in; we can get you to shore." But he refused and said, "No, the Lord will protect me." But the waters continued to rise up to the second floor, and another larger boat made its way to his window. "Climb out," they said. "We'll get you to safety." But he refused and said, "No, the Lord will protect me." The rains continued, and he climbed out onto the roof as a helicopter swooped down and dropped a ladder as a crew member yelled, "Get on the ladder; you will be saved." But he refused and said, "No, the Lord will protect me." The waters continued to rise and consumed him, and he drowned. He appeared in heaven before the Lord, and the man said, "Lord, how could you fail me? I put my faith in you, and yet I drowned." And the Lord said, in that deeply resonating voice we all attribute to God but with some resignation in it, "Good grief, what do you want me to do? I sent you two boats and a helicopter."

That is the third part of the Serenity Prayer. *The Wisdom to Know the Difference.* I recently read an article by the Dalai Lama where he wrote, "…religious people should pay more attention to scientists rather than just pray, pray, pray." Pray, certainly, if that is your way, and remember that God helps those who help themselves. You remember that old saying, don't you? Remember as well John Kennedy's admonition that "God's work on earth must surely be our own."

I'm reminded of a poem, "Invictus," that I have written about before, but it bears repeating.

Invictus

Out of the night that covers me,

Black as the Pit from pole to pole,

I thank whatever gods may be

For my unconquerable soul.

In the fell clutch of circumstance

I have not winced nor cried aloud.

Under the bludgeoning of chance

Thorns Have Roses

My head is bloody, but unbowed.

Beyond this place of wrath and tears

Looms but the Horror of the Shade,

And yet the menace of the years

Finds, and shall find, me unafraid.

It matters not how strait the gate,

How charged with punishments the scroll.

I am the master of my fate:

I am the captain of my soul.

~**William Ernest Henley**

So what are we to do with this tension between Faith and Action?

Two thoughts come to my mind. One is to pray if that is your way. The second is to act on those circumstances that lie within our control. Two prayers came to me recently. One through an "Oldies" station from the Youngbloods in 1967 when they sang,

Come on people now

Smile on your brother

Everybody get together

Try to love one another – right now.

I'm willing to pray for that. My wife, Marie, gave me a handwritten note and said, "You might want to use this in your chapter." It comes from an AARP article.

Let us all unite to create a society that values

Hope over Hate

Faith over Fear

and

Compassion over Confrontation.

I'm willing to pray that prayer too.

Courage, of course, is not the absence of fear. It is, rather, acting even though one is afraid. Upon what shall we act? Here's a thought. Do as you will, so long as you hurt no one. Seems awfully open-ended, yet the great religions of the world are agreed upon this single recommendation. The Buddhists say, "Hurt not others with that which pains yourself." The Christians write, "Do unto others as you would have them do unto you." Hinduism teaches, "Treat others as you would yourself be treated." Islam proclaims, "Do unto all men as you would wish to have done unto you." Judaism instructs, "What you yourself hate, do to no man." And Native Americans tutor, "Live in harmony, for we are all related." It really isn't that we don't know what to do. It is far more likely that we often lack the will to act on what we know to be this universal truth.

There is an Essay/Poem that I very much like—you are likely to have heard of it and even to have read it. It is "Desiderata" (it means something that is needed or wanted/desired) by Max Ehrmann. Ponder these thoughts as something like a course of action in this trying world. "Go placidly amid the noise and haste." In the arguments and discourse, take what you like and leave the rest. "Be on good terms with all persons." I have written elsewhere if you want to be loved, learn to love others. Those who choose to be happy must let others find their happiness as the welfare of each of us is intertwined with the welfare of all. If you can accept the shortfalls of others, the windfall for you is a happier life. "Take kindly the counsel of the years." Growing old isn't for sissies and yet we have not lived all these years for nothing. We know that things pass. Old age gives us, if nothing else, perspective. "Do not stress yourself with imaginings." Life itself is tough enough without making stuff up. Let's turn to that eminent philosopher of life, Sherlock Holmes, for a bit of wisdom here. "It is a capital mistake to theorize before one has data. Insensibly one begins to twist facts to suit theories, instead of theories to suit facts." (Sir Arthur Conan Doyle). "Beyond a wholesome discipline, be gentle with yourself" is neither a recommendation to pursue pleasure nor a strict admonition for a moral absolute. It asks us to neither beat ourselves up in pursuit of perfection nor to slide into slovenly disregard.

I recognize that these somewhat vague guidelines can be seen as "sugar-coated sentiments." There can clearly be a time for righteous indignation at the social injustice we see, and that is a time for moral action. Yet, one of the teachings of age itself is that one cannot live one's life in a state of agitation, and the principles of daily life are far more moderate than the principles of indignant righteousness. Therefore, as Ehrmann concludes, "Be at peace with God whatever you conceive Him to be." As a seeker once asked of a mountain-top sage, "How many Gods are there?" The Sage replied, "How many people are there?" So without getting stuck in that particular mire, let us say, so far as daily life is concerned, "Be at peace."

A final word here about faith, prayer, meditation, and contemplation. Action without faith (in its broadest context) is anemic, tepid, and half-hearted. We swim toward the shore with, at minimum, the hope that we will reach it.

Time to close, and let us let a poet lead us to the end.

Pandemic

What if you thought of it

as the Jews consider the Sabbath—

the most sacred of times?

Cease from travel.

Cease from buying and selling.

Give up, just for now,

on trying to make the world

different than it is.

Sing. Pray. Touch only those

to whom you commit your life.

Center down.

And when your body has become still,

reach out with your heart.

Know that we are connected

in ways that are terrifying and beautiful.

(You could hardly deny it now.)

Thorns Have Roses

Know that our lives

are in one another's hands.

(Surely, that has come clear.)

Do not reach out your hands.

Reach out your heart.

Reach out your words.

Reach out all the tendrils

of compassion that move, invisibly,

where we cannot touch.

Promise this world your love.

~Lynn Ungar, 3/11/20

Thorns Have Roses

a
WISHES

We spend our lives in wishes

And no Genie comes to make them true

We meet a wish and see the sky

To touch some need

To heal some wound

To soothe some ache

And pass it up to live a lonely time wishing

What power is there that could give us

The strength

The courage

The will

To choose life over wishes

Would it that our lives were spent

Thorns Have Roses

In the living

In the loving

In the joy and sorrow

That would have made a good wish

We spend out lives in wishes

And no Genie comes to make them true.

9
I KNOW A WAY OUT OF HELL

What follows might seem a challenge to the beliefs of many, but it isn't intended to be that. It is an exploration of ideas. Now, I'm not going to try to fool anyone here. I have a preference for some of these ideas over others, but all can be held with equal sincerity, and I am content with that. I'm going to give you a little bit of Hell just a brief visit to explore just what we mean when we are talking about Hell.

Here is a short story: A man dies and goes to hell. Satan greets him, shows him three doors, and says, "You must spend the rest of eternity in one of the rooms behind these doors. Look in each one and decide which one you want." The man opens the first door and sees a bunch of people standing on their heads on a wooden floor, looking very uncomfortable. He opens the second door and sees a bunch of people balanced on a slender pole on one leg above a flaming pit looking even more uncomfortable. Finally, he opens the third door and sees a bunch of people standing around chatting and drinking coffee, up to their knees in manure. "Hmmm," he says, "that looks bad, but it's better than the other two. I'll take the third door." Satan smiles and shows him in. Ten minutes later, Satan walks back into the room and says, "All right, coffee break's over, everyone back on your heads."

Let's face it, Hell isn't a pleasant place in the best of definitions. But, it does have several definitions. In fact, if you were to undertake a study of Hell, you would soon be overwhelmed. It is, as you might suspect, a dark, murky, confusing, and confounding subject. You might spend a lifetime of study and not emerge with a satisfying conclusion. So my humble efforts here aren't aimed at ending the debate but only to set the stage to talk about a way out of Hell.

Old Testament

The word "hell" occurs 31 times in the Old Testament. All 31 of those times, the word translated as hell is the

Hebrew word Sheol (Shee-OO). While the English word "hell" has connotations as a place of punishment for the condemned, Sheol does not have such connotations.

New Testament

The term "hell" is found 23 times in the King James Version of the English Bible. There is a great deal of confusion among religious folks regarding this word since the English form "hell" actually represents three different terms in the Greek New Testament.

Interestingly, in 40 accepted translations of the Holy Bible in the Old Testament, Hell is mentioned in only 2: the Authorized KJV and the New KJV. Of the 40, only 12 mention hell in the New Testament. The word "heaven" appears in the Bible over 550 times.

Traditional Christian Views On Hell

There is the traditional view that has dominated Christendom for the last 1500 years. It is that of "eternal conscious torment" for all those who do not "accept Jesus Christ as Lord and Savior" in this life. After death, there is no longer any hope considered for them. "Hell" is defined as the place in which unbelievers "suffer everlasting conscious punishment away from the presence of God."

A Christian view might be as follows: Those who die without Jesus Christ will stand for eternity in a place where the fire is not quenched. If Gandhi did not trust Jesus Christ before he died, then he is in hell tonight. The Buddha, for all his wisdom, is in hell. This awful place called hell. You have committed sins against God, and because of your sin, there is a terrible penalty to be paid. The way out of this hell is acceptance of Jesus Christ as your personal Savior. This is an individual act of sincere repentance—and is for yourself alone. Christian theology then goes on into many varieties of creeds to which one must accept and adhere, such as the Nicene Creed, for example.

Jesus himself was not tied to the idea of exclusive adherence to a single doctrine. In the Book of Mark (9:38-41), John says, "Teacher, we saw a man using your name to force demons out of a person. He is not one of us. So we told him to stop because he does not belong to our group." Jesus said, "Don't stop him. Any person that uses my name to do powerful things will not soon say bad things about me.

The person that is not against us is with us. I tell you the truth. If a person helps you by giving you a drink of water because you belong to Christ, then that person will truly get his reward.

Unitarian-Universalists

There are other views. Perhaps you are unaware that I created Universalism on August 8, 1971. Some of you might have another view of the history of Universalism, but for me, I developed it independently on that date, the date of our first son's birth. I held his small, fragile body as tenderly as I could, and I knew in that moment that in this creation of Marie's and my love for one another, no loving father would condemn his son to everlasting Hell as we have described above. No such place could exist in the heart of a loving parent.

In giving up my early teachings of salvation, I felt alone and spiritually isolated and yet determined that I must have been misled. It only came to me later that others held similar views. I discovered the Unitarian-Universalists, and while they are described as the church with no theology and believe anything, that is, of course, nonsense. A core belief is that each of us must find a theology, God, or a life path to which we can commit ourselves. The Unitarian Universalist Association is organized around seven principles which member churches and individual members "covenant" (agree) to "affirm and promote." I invite you to Google those seven principles if you wish to know more. In general, this question for Universalists of what lies beyond isn't of much import; it is a given. For example, 1 Corinthians 15:22, "For as in Adam all die, so in Christ all will be made alive."

Remember earlier, I said that the traditional view of Hell had dominated Christianity for the last 1500 years. Well, actually, that's kind of interesting, isn't it? Because 1500 years doesn't get us up to the present. There are roughly 500 years unaccounted for, and it is in those 500 years after Christ's death that Universalism was, in fact, a widely accepted belief among Christians.

Universal Salvation is the theological position that God will save all of humanity. Today's world news is saturated with the tragedies resulting from religions that insist on their own "exclusive" path to God. Some are so straight and narrow as to become a razor that cuts so fine that it severs human beings from one another. Universalists are reasserting the relevance of that loving doctrine known to the earliest Christians. Salvation is a gift for everyone.

Some assert that there isn't one exclusive path to God but that religion is like a stained glass window through which the light shines and the light refracts in this direction and that with a touch of purple here and a gleam of gold there, a splash of orange over there, and a dash of chartreuse here. Each is different, but all stem from a single light. How did we get so off track? Well, part of the answer appears to be that old bugaboo, "Translation." Universalists do not reject the undeniable fact that Hell is in the Bible but hold that what has come down to us isn't an accurate reflection of what both the Old and the New Testaments teach about Hell and Salvation. Nor in today's world do Unitarian-Universalists reject the idea that meanness, cruelty, and evil do exist in the world and that consequences should and do follow. As I wrote previously, Our human history is teeming with scoundrels and zealots, lunatics, and monsters whose contribution to humanity has damaged lives, ravaged communities, and dysfunctional societies that responsible and caring people have had to spend their lives repairing. And yet, one of the essential tenets of Universalism is that all punishment in Hell is remedial, curative, and purifying. So where did all this "Eternal" and "Everlasting" and "Unending" condemnation come from? It is a mistranslation again.

Translation/Mistranslation of the Scriptures from Greek to Latin contributed to the reinterpretation of the nature of Hell. The Greek "aion" (in English, "eon") is an indefinite period of time, usually of long duration. When it was translated into the Latin Vulgate, "aion" became "aeternam" (E-Turn-Um), which means "eternal." These translation errors were the basis for much of what was written about Eternal Hell. Frankly, the word "hell," given its popular understanding now, is not the best word to use. One phrase that Jesus himself used is "aionios kolasis" (Eye-On-Knee-Oss) (Ko-Lass-Ess), which in New Testament Greek means "age-lasting correction." In Matthew 25:46, Jesus warns that people who do not show compassion to the poor and suffering in this life will enter into an age (aionios)

(Eye-On-Knee-Oss) of corrective judgment (kolasis) (Ko-Lass-Ess), while others are enjoying an age of divine life (aionios zoe) (Eye-On-Knee-Oss) (Zo-EEE). Unfortunately, this verse in the Bible is usually translated as "eternal punishment" rather than the correct understanding of the Greek, which would be a punishment that is reformative, not vindictive, and only for a limited period of time. Mistranslations such as this one are common in most popular versions of the Bible, leading Christians to think that eternal hell is a true teaching of Christianity. By far, the main person responsible for making Hell eternal in the Western Church was St. Augustine. He did not know Greek and had tried to study it but stated that he hated it. Sadly, it is his misunderstanding of Greek that cemented the concept of Eternal Hell in the Western Church. Augustine not only said that Hell was eternal for the wicked but also for anyone who wasn't a Christian. What was an "eon" in the Greek Original became "eternal" in Latin and, of course, came down to us in the King James Version of the Bible.

What Does This Get Us?

"So what does all this get us? It might boil down to a question. If someone were to ask me, 'Do you believe in Heaven and Hell?' I would probably answer, 'Yes, but it isn't a question of 'Where' but of 'When.' 'Heaven' and 'Hell' are best understood not as humanity's destination after death, but as realities in this world. Social Justice is our act of concerning itself with the real and the concrete as we take seriously the actual world we live in..." (The Unitarian Universalist Pocket Guide).

In the movie "Gandhi," war is raging between the Muslims and the Hindus, and Gandhi has undertaken a fast until the violence ends. A crowd of Hindus breaks in on Gandhi. He is weak and close to death, and all are pleading with Gandhi to end his fast and save his life. They vow to end the fighting, and Gandhi blesses them. But then one of the mob breaks through and throws a piece of bread at Gandhi and shouts:

Rioter: Eat, Eat! - I am going to hell but not with your death on my soul.

Gandhi: Only God decides who goes to hell.

Rioter: I killed a child.

Gandhi: Why?

Rioter: They killed my son, my boy. The Muslims killed my child.

Gandhi: I know a way out of hell. Find a child - a child whose mother and father have been killed. A little boy about this high. Raise him as your own, only make sure he is a Muslim and raise him as one.

We know that Hell can be on earth and that there are those among us who suffer, are denied, mistreated, hunger, and endure painful and deprived lives. Mother Teresa recognized this and reminded us of the work to do on earth. She said, "The other night I dreamt I went to the gates of Heaven, and St. Peter said, 'Go back to earth. There are no slums up here.'"

What we do here matters.

> Like Gandhi – I know a way out of Hell.
>
> And I saw the river
>
> over which every soul must pass

to reach the kingdom of heaven

and the name of that river was suffering:

and I saw a boat that carries souls across the river

and the name of that boat was Love.

~St. John of the Cross

What Jesus spoke so many lives ago remains true today. "If I speak in the tongues of men or of angels, but do not have love, I am only a resounding gong or a clanging cymbal. If I have the gift of prophecy and can fathom all mysteries and all knowledge, and if I have a faith that can move mountains, but do not have love, I am nothing. If I give all I possess to the poor and give over my body to hardship that I may boast, but do not have love, I gain nothing." (1 Corinthians 13 New International Version (NIV).

Here is a thought:

What if you slept? And what if, In your sleep, You dreamed?

And what if, In your dream, You went to Heaven

And there plucked A strange and Beautiful flower?

And what if, When you awoke, You had the flower In your hand?

Ah, what then?

~Samuel Taylor Coleridge

Here is another story that many of you may have heard already but still teach. Another dream, and in the dream, a man is led to two doors. He opens one and sees within a table set with abundant food and people with three-foot-long utensils with which they could spear the food but could not place it into their mouths and so they were emaciated, starving, and miserable. The Man asked, "What place is this?" and the Guide answered, "This is Hell." The guide opened the second door and the room was identical. The people again held long utensils with which they could spear the food and yet the people seemed happy and robust and the man asked, "What place is this?" and the Guide answered, "This is Heaven." The man protested and said "But they are the same! Why is one Hell and one Heaven?"

The Guide replied, "Because in Heaven the people have learned to feed one another." Here is a poem.

Abou Ben Adhem

Abou Ben Adhem (may his tribe increase!)
Awoke one night from a deep dream of peace,
And saw, within the moonlight in his room, making it rich,
and like a lily in bloom, an angel writing in a book of gold:
Exceeding peace had made Ben Adhem bold,
And to the Presence in the room, he said
"What writest thou?"—
The vision raised its head
And with a look made of all sweet accord,
Answered "The names of those who love the Lord."
"And is mine one?" said Abou.
"Nay, not so," replied the angel.
Abou spoke more low, but cheerily still, and said

> "I pray thee, then, Write me as one that loves his fellow men."
>
> The angel wrote and vanished.
>
> The next night It came again with a great wakening light,
>
> And showed the names whom love of God had blessed,
>
> And lo! Ben Adhem's name led all the rest.

Let me end with this. An American Psychologist, Abraham Maslow, whose major work had to do with the healthy personality, those human beings who were navigating life in a positive, contributing way not overpowered by the travails of life but accepting of who they are, competent, widely identified, and aligned with others. Maslow once said a practical and moving thing. He said, "Every time you do something to raise a person up, every time you positively affirm another in some way, no matter how small, you are an influence in their chance to have a meaningful life." When you do that, you are walking the path out of Hell.

Thorns Have Roses

10
WOULD JESUS WEAR A ROLEX? POVERTY, WEALTH AND OUR SPIRITUAL WELL BEING

I'm exploring a serious idea, but in a pretty light way, and in my lightness, I'm not mocking anyone or questioning anyone's beliefs. I'm asking a question, and it's a puzzler: What is the role of wealth in our spiritual life?

Which reminds me of a story. Poor Bob Clancy lived alone with only a pet dog for company. One day, the dog died, and Clancy went to the parish priest and asked, "Father, my dog is dead. Could you say a mass for the poor creature?" Father Patrick replied, "I'm afraid not; we cannot have services for an animal in the church. But there are some

Liberal Heathens down the road, and there's no telling what they believe. Maybe they'll do something for the creature." Clancy said, "I'll go right away, Father. Do you think $10,000 is enough to donate to them for the service?" Father Patrick exclaimed, "Sweet Mary, Mother of Jesus! Why didn't you tell me the dog was Catholic?"

What's to learn from this? Well, money talks! And the Church has ears.

The watch wasn't invented until around the 15th century and was mostly worn by women as a pendant. Then, the First World War came along with the need to coordinate artillery and infantry attacks, and all that, and so the need for timing became more and more necessary. Army contractors began to issue reliable, cheap, mass-produced wristwatches, which were ideal for these purposes. When the war ended, demobilized European and American officers were allowed to keep their wristwatches and brought them home, and so now we have wristwatches.

So, wristwatches weren't even around in Jesus's time and the question of "Would Jesus wear a Rolex?" is nonsense, or, perhaps, in our case here today, a metaphorical question.

Here's a satirical song written by Margaret Archer and Chet Atkins probing that question of the role of wealth in our lives.

Would Jesus Wear a Rolex?

Woke up this mornin', turned on the T.V. set.

there in livin' color, was somethin' I can't forget.

This man was preachin' at me, layin' on the charm

askin' me for twenty, with ten-thousand on his arm.

He wore designer clothes, and a big smile on his face

sellin' me salvation while they sang Amazin' Grace.

Askin' me for money, when he had all the signs of wealth.

I almost wrote a check out, but then I asked myself

Would He wear a pinky ring, would He drive a fancy car?

> Would His wife wear furs and diamonds, would His dressin' room have a star?
>
> If He came back tomorrow, well there's somethin' I'd like to know
>
> Could ya tell me, Would Jesus wear a Rolex on His television show?

The Bible contains more than 300 verses on the poor, social justice, and God's deep concern for both. I have some good news for you! We are not going to review every one of them! I'm just going to focus on the New Testament.

A central issue for Religious folks is the role money plays in our lives. There are numerous warnings against wealth as well as many blessings for the poor.

We know that Jesus was a blue-collar worker, a laborer, a peasant and not a noble; a man of humble origins and was not born into a family of high social standing.

It is likely that he had the normal suspicions of the poor about the rich and had seen, felt, and experienced the ordinary humiliations of the poor in their dealings with the rich, including the expectation of subordination, deference, and, indeed, dependence on the rich for their very sustenance.

Jesus came as a poor man. There's all sorts of meaning in that, but at the very least, we can say that Jesus took the issue of poverty personally. A church or a nation that ignores its poor or places stumbling blocks in their way, whose supreme God is money, is very far from the spirit of God in Jesus's way.

It is clear from the gospels that Jesus has a profound fondness and love for the poor of the earth and stern warnings for the rich.

This is, perhaps, the most well-known. *"It is easier for a camel to go through the eye of a needle than for a rich person to enter the kingdom of God."*

One explanation of the "Eye of the Needle" is that Jerusalem was a walled city that closed its gates at night, but caravans would arrive after dark and needed to enter the city. Small entry gates were built. One of these was the "Eye of the Needle." It was large enough to admit a single man but far too small for a loaded camel. So the camels had to be unloaded, the goods carried inside, and the camel would then have to be put down on its knees and crawl, be pushed and pulled through the gate. This illustrates the difficulty of getting a camel through the eye of the needle. It was challenging but not impossible, as we shall see later.

What does it mean "to enter the Kingdom of God?" Some say it means salvation, eternal life for our souls. Others might consider it a metaphor. Entering the Kingdom of God means being close to God, being whole, at peace, and at home with ourselves.

So, why is it so difficult for the rich?

"People who want to get rich fall into temptation and a trap and into many foolish and harmful desires that plunge men into ruin and destruction. For the love of money is the root of all kinds of evil. Some people, eager for money, have wandered from the faith and pierced themselves with many griefs." (1 Timothy 6:9-10)

Jesus was not gentle in his condemnation of money and its effect on spiritual wholeness. When it was almost time for the Jewish Passover, Jesus went to Jerusalem. In the temple courts, he found people selling cattle, sheep, and doves and others sitting at tables exchanging money. So he made a whip out of cords and drove all from the temple courts, both sheep and cattle. He scattered the coins of the money changers and overturned their tables. (John 2:13-15 NIV)

Note: Why were they exchanging coins, and what were they exchanging them for? The Jews held that coins other than Hebrew coins weren't proper in the Temple, so people had to exchange Roman or other currency for Hebrew coins to be acceptable.

My house shall be called the house of prayer, but you have made it a den of thieves.

Get Out! Get out! Do not make my Father's house a marketplace. (Matthew 21:12)

It would be as if churches installed an ATM, a branch of the Bank of America, or an office for Payday Loan. Jesus said, "This is God's house." It is God's Hospital where we come to have our souls healed. Jesus was angry, more angry than anywhere else in the New Testament.

Also, for the first time, He made a claim to a special relationship with God. "This is my Father's house."

No one can serve two masters. Either he will hate the one and love the other, or he will be devoted to the one and despise the other. You cannot serve both God and Money." (Matthew 6:24)

For where your treasure is, there your heart will be also."

I remember an image I came across in college. I had read Steinbeck's "The Grapes of Wrath," and one of the images toward the end of the book is the Joad family, along with Rose of Sharon (great with child), trapped in a boxcar with the floodwaters rising. I was working on a term paper for a sociology class, so I went down into the stacks of the library and searched out some old magazines from the 1930s, like the Saturday Evening Post. I found a photograph of a family in a boxcar surrounded by floodwaters. I also came across another photo: a photograph in California of a huge mound of oranges being burned surrounded by armed police, with migrant farm workers (remember the "Okies") starving and prevented from eating surplus oranges. Who would do such a thing, and why? The answer was to keep the price of oranges high so growers could realize a greater profit.

A major aircraft manufacturer's Corporate Board was informed of a defect in the design of a recreational aircraft which had resulted in crashes and the deaths of the pilots and passengers. The Board voted not to inform the public or correct the defect. Why? The answer was that after the Board's action was exposed, the costs of the recall and repair of the defect would exceed the costs of settling the claims of the lawsuits brought for wrongful death. What master is served here?

This could be a whole chapter all by itself, but I have to be content here with these examples. I invite you to Google or look up "Worst Ethical Business Decisions in History." I suspect you will be as angry as Jesus in the Temple.

So, what is the remedy?

And, behold, one came and said unto him, Good Master, what good thing shall I do, that I may have eternal life?

And he said unto him, Why callest thou me good? there is none good but one, that is, God: but if thou wilt enter into life, keep the commandments.

He saith unto him, Which? Jesus said, Thou shalt do no murder, Thou shalt not commit adultery, Thou shalt not steal, Thou shalt not bear false witness, Honor thy father and thy mother: and, Thou shalt love thy neighbor as thyself.

Jesus's straightforward reply was "Keep the Commandments."

But that wasn't enough for the rich man who said:

The young man saith unto him, All these things have I kept from my youth up: what lack I yet?

Jesus said unto him, If thou wilt be perfect, go and sell all that thou hast, and give to the poor, and thou shalt have treasure in heaven: and come and follow me.

And this as well —*Sell your possessions, and give to the needy*

And they were selling their possessions and belongings and distributing the proceeds to all, as any had need.

So the command to be poor! To live our lives in poverty. Bummer, that's just too hard, and we aren't going to do it. Actually, not really. Jesus doesn't ask us to be poor. This reply was to a specific request of how to live an essentially monastic life, the life Jesus and the Disciples were living.

Two things we need to remember about Jesus. First, he was an apocalyptic preacher who believed the Kingdom of God was coming, and soon, so giving up stuff didn't matter all that much since it wouldn't be long before the Kingdom of God was on earth. We have to remember that Jesus was an Ascetic, used to denial of personal needs, a beggar, and relied upon the gifts of others to practice his ministry.

Jesus and his Disciples had a ministry that was supported by others. Mary Magdalene, who has to be the most maligned woman in the Bible, has had various false images attributed to her, including prostitute, groupie, camp follower, Jesus lover/wife, sexy, and beguiling – all of which are untrue or certainly unsupported by the Gospels. It is written that Jesus cast out seven devils from Mary, not spiritual devils but physical devils, something like epilepsy or seizures. This is an example of faith healing, followed by reverence and support from Mary.

In some recent things, I have read about Mary Magdalene, which means Mary of Magdala, a place, may well have been more a contemporary of Mary, the Mother of Jesus, than of Jesus himself. One idea is that she was a person of means and not only a follower of Jesus but a financial supporter of Jesus' ministry. She was a single woman from another area, Magdala, on her own and, hence, a person of property and of independent means. She was, perhaps, a patron and a financial supporter of Jesus' ministry.

The apostolic group was ministered to both financially and physically by several women, who took care of tasks such as cooking and washing, and Mary was among them.

Then there was Joseph of Arimathea. He was described as an "honorable counselor," meaning he was a member of the Jewish Sanhedrin. Joseph was a rich man and a disciple of Jesus. Upon hearing of Jesus' death, this secret disciple of Jesus "went boldly unto Pilate and requested the body of Jesus." Pilate, after confirmation of Jesus' death by a centurion, allowed Joseph's request. Joseph immediately purchased fine linen (Mark 15:46) and proceeded to Golgotha to take the body of Jesus down from the cross. There, according to John 19:39, Joseph and Nicodemus took the body, wrapped it in the fine linen, and applied the myrrh and aloes Nicodemus had brought. Golgotha is the Hill of Skulls because those who died on the cross were left there to rot, not taken down and buried so Joseph's request was unusual, and that Pilate granted it perhaps shows the regard in which Joseph was held as well as Nicodemus (a Pharisee and a member of the Sanhedrin).

Zacchaeus was the chief among the publicans, and he was rich.

And he sought to see Jesus who he was; and could not for the press, because he was little of stature. (Zacchaeus was a wee little man)

And he ran before and climbed up into a sycamore tree to see him: for he was to pass that way.

And when Jesus came to the place, he looked up, and saw him, and said unto him, Zacchaeus, make haste, and come down; for today I must abide at thy house.

And he made haste and came down, and received him joyfully.

And Zacchaeus stood, and said unto the Lord: Behold, Lord, the half of my goods I give to the poor; and if I have taken anything from any man by false accusation, I restore him fourfold.

And Jesus said unto him, This day is salvation come to this house.

These are wealthy people, supporters of Jesus, respected by Jesus and not condemned by him.

So if we are not called to be poor and yet Jesus is suspicious of the rich and condemning of elevating money above spiritual well-being, then what is the remedy? What should we do about money, wealth, and our spiritual well-being?

They are to do good, to be rich in good works, to be generous and ready to share, thus storing up treasure for themselves as a good foundation for the future, so that they may take hold of that which is truly life.

Here's a thought attributed to John Wesley -Do all the good you can. By all the means you can. In all the ways you can. In all the places you can. At all times you can. To all the people you can. As long as ever you can."

In fact, there are roughly 63 Bible verses that deal directly with Generosity. We're going to review them all. Just kidding, but here are a couple.

I do not mean that others should be eased and you burdened, but that as a matter of fairness, your abundance at the present time should supply their need, so that their abundance may supply your need, that there may be fairness. (2 Corinthians 8:13)

You will be enriched in every way to be generous in every way. (2 Corinthians 9:11)

And not Generosity for Show.

As for the rich in this present age, charge them not to be haughty, nor to set their hopes on the uncertainty of riches.

"Thus, when you give to the needy, sound no trumpet before you, as the hypocrites do in the synagogues and in the streets, that they may be praised by others. Truly, I say to you, they have received their reward. But when you give to the needy, do not let your left hand know what your right hand is doing, so that your giving may be in secret. And your Father who sees in secret will reward you. (Matthew 6:2)

Erik Erikson had a theory of stages of life development. One of the later ones is labeled Generativity versus

Stagnation. Contributing to society and doing things to benefit future generations are important needs at the generativity versus stagnation stage of development. Generativity refers to "making your mark" on the world through caring for others, creating things, and accomplishing things that make the world a better place. Generativity is a goal of social responsibility for the next generation and contrasts with the narrow interest in yourself and being self-absorbed. Generativity is an extension of love into the future. It is a concern for the next generation and for all future generations.

Consider teaching, writing, invention, the arts and the sciences, social activism, and contributing to the welfare of future generations as forms of generativity.

To answer the question – would Jesus wear a Rolex?

Consider this:

They like to walk around in flowing robes and love to be greeted in the marketplaces and have the most important seats in the synagogues and the places of honor at banquets. They devour widows' houses and for a show make lengthy prayers.

And he sat down opposite the treasury and watched the people putting money into the offering box. Many rich people put in large sums. And a poor widow came and put in two small copper coins, which make a penny. And he called his disciples to him and said to them, "Truly, I say to you, this poor widow has put in more than all those who are contributing to the offering box. For they all contributed out of their abundance, but she out of her poverty has put in everything she had, all she had to live on." (Mark 12: 42 – 44)

So, no, Jesus would not wear a Rolex. He would probably wear a Timex. He would recommend that we avoid ostentatiousness, be generous, and dampen the flames of Hell here on earth as best we can. Now that we've settled the notion of whether or not Jesus would wear a Rolex – more likely a Timex – one last question is before us. Would He drive a fancy car?

We know that the only form of transportation Jesus used, other than walking, was once on the eve of Passover when entering Jerusalem. "Saying unto them, 'Go into the village, and straightway ye shall find an ass tied, and bring it unto me.' And the disciples went, and brought the ass, and they set him thereon."

Thorns Have Roses

So, just as Jesus would more likely wear a Timex rather than a Rolex, he wouldn't be likely to drive a Rolls-Royce, but a car more common to the people.

So, let's see: open-air transportation, a popularly used mode of transportation, and named after an equine. I don't want you to think I'm overly influenced by the car Marie and I drive, which is a modest Mustang Convertible, but Jesus, riding a donkey out in the open air extrapolated into the future... I'm just saying.

11
FIVE SMOOTH STONES

I'm going to tell you a story. It is a story you already know. It comes from the Bible in the Book of Samuel, Chapter 17. It is the story of David and Goliath.

Now it came to pass in the rule of Saul, the King of the Israelites, that the Philistines gathered their army for war and drew up their battle line at the Valley of Elah. The Israelites on one side of the valley, and the Philistines on the other. Among the Philistines was a giant named Goliath, his height was 6 cubits and a span (a cubit being roughly 18 inches or more than 9 feet tall), who came out and challenged the Israelites, saying, "Send forth a champion, and if he defeats me, then the Philistines will be the slaves of the Israelites."

When Saul and his army heard these words, their knees shook, and they trembled in fear, and none would go out. David was a shepherd boy whose brothers were in Saul's army. David had gone to visit them and to take them food. He heard Goliath's challenge. He also heard that there would be a substantial reward for anyone who defeated Goliath. David took it upon himself to fight the giant. We might question his motives, which might have been part financial and part something like tribal pride or perhaps even religious fervor. Perhaps he felt the presence of his Lord God. His brothers and the other soldiers of Saul's army mocked him, saying, "You are nothing but a boy." David said, "I have protected my flock from bears and wolves with my staff and sling." Good enough for Saul, who accepted him and said, "Go." Saul gave David his own armor, but it was too unwieldy for David. He threw off the armor and went down to a stream where he chose five (5) smooth stones.

When Goliath came out the next day, David walked out to meet him. Goliath cursed him and charged. David ran toward him, reached into his bag, and drew out one smooth stone, flung it, striking the Philistine in the forehead. The stone sank deep and Goliath fell face down on the ground. David had done what no one else in Saul's army would do. He had faced his fears and, in facing them, defeated them.

I guess caution is needed here. As it turns out, David might not be the greatest role model for us to follow, given that he went on to make some questionable decisions about how to live his own life. But in this moment, this story of David and Goliath can serve as a metaphor for life and challenges. Armed with the proper tools, we can meet our challenges and deal with them, perhaps even beat them.

We are going to reach into the stream and draw out five smooth stones that have the promise of helping us in life as we face the challenges and obstacles of our daily lives — a small toolbox to help us cope. What are the five (5) smooth stones we might use to face the obstacles of our lives?

Love

Here is our First Stone, Love. I'm going to take a little wisdom from a rock and roll song written by Lou Adler, Herb Alpert, and Sam Cooke.

Don't know much about history

Don't know much biology

Don't know much about my science book

But I do know that I love you

And I know that if you love me too

What a wonderful world this would be

Um Um Um Um – What a wonderful world ... this could be.

This song can have special meaning for us with a slight tweak of definitional understanding. Love is one of those words that not only varies in meaning from person to person but can even change its meaning for the same person in different contexts. For example, when I say, "I love my parents," that doesn't mean the same thing as when I say, "I love my wife," which, in turn, differs from when I say, "I love our children." It's nothing like what I mean when I say, "I love John Steinbeck."

I offer this definition of Love: "The co-equal right to live and prosper." It implies a willingness to share in the joys and sorrows of humanity, to do what we can when we can, and to help when help is needed and wanted.

I ask you to remember that definition because we are going to come back to it. As simple as it is, it is a powerful motivating and societal force. It unifies us but can also separate us, depending on whether one believes in the power of love or sees other forces as more central to human relationships, such as money, power, privilege, or status. Of course, cynics don't appreciate love much; they consider it naive and often lack happiness in their relationships. Go figure.

Yet, we do know that "Love," in its many definitions, has launched ships, started wars, led to atrocities, and created villains and heroes who sacrificed their lives and fortunes for humanity's sake. In our social definition of love, we have committed ourselves to "Stand on the side of love" to affirm and promote our principles of dignity, justice, compassion, truth, the democratic process, and our planetary interdependence. Love serves as the foundation in the toolbox necessary to face our fears and obstacles in life.

Hope

Our second stone is "Hope." In Greek Mythology, Prometheus defied the gods by stealing fire and giving it to humanity, an act that enabled progress and civilization.

Prometheus is known as a champion of humankind. However, Zeus, the highest-ranking God, was not pleased with Prometheus's rebellion and punished him with eternal torment. Zeus had Prometheus chained to a rock where he was attacked each day by an eagle that clawed him open and ate his liver. Since Prometheus was immortal, he lived on only to be attacked each day throughout eternity. Out of this myth, another is created - the Myth of Pandora and Pandora's Box.

Pandora, the first woman created by the Gods, was brought into existence as part of the punishment of Prometheus and given as a gift to Prometheus's brother. In his house, out of curiosity, she opened a jar/box left in his care containing War, Crime, Famine, Pestilence, Cruelty, Malice, Woe, Wickedness, and even Death. She released all the evils of humankind, what we might call the Four Horsemen of the Apocalypse in our Judeo-Christian tradition: War, Pestilence, Famine, and Death. However, for all the evils that escaped, something remained in the box. It was one last "gift" for humankind, and that last gift was "HOPE."

It's worth repeating: For all the human hardships contained in the box, the last treasure in the box was Hope.

Now, let's consider definitions and meanings. Hope isn't optimism. Optimism is the belief that this world is the best of all possible worlds, the conviction that good must ultimately prevail over evil in the universe. Hope isn't a belief that everything will turn out for the best. It isn't the naive, wishful thinking that hardened realists mock and ridicule. It is, in fact, a factual, even hard-nosed reality of life. It is the understanding that the future is unknown.

The fact of the matter is that we are no strangers to Hope at all. We live it in our daily lives, in our ordinary interactions with one another, and even in something as simple as a trip to the grocery store. I live in a large city where driving an automobile is not something one should take for granted. We have some challenging drivers, but I do hope that everyone will stay in their lane, stop appropriately, and yield the right of way. It isn't a given, but we are reliably able to get to the store and purchase goods, which we hope are safe. We count on literally hundreds, perhaps thousands, of people unknown to us to grow, transport, clean, and deliver every item we bring home. This is the foundation of a society, and we hope that each of us can be counted on to do what is asked of us to make society work. Those who do not are, of course, called criminals. When they cheat, rob, steal, or harm others, we learn about it in the news.

I don't know if you've ever considered why the news always seems to be bad. Airplane accidents aren't common, family disputes typically don't end in violence, banks aren't routinely robbed, and our homes aren't invaded regularly. These things do happen, and when they do, we are shocked, saddened, and even surprised because they are out of the ordinary. Hence, it becomes news. Bad news is reported precisely because it is news. The vast majority of people live up to our hopes and fulfill our hope and faith in them. Those who do not are the exception, and therefore, they are the news. Bad things do happen, and good people have to cope. One of the tools they have is hope. The word isn't written, and it is within that unknown future that our actions might have an influence on the outcome. Hope is the impetus for action.

Courage

Our third stone is Courage. In Milton's "Paradise Lost," he writes, "The mind is its own place, and in itself can make a Heaven of Hell, a Hell of Heaven." In these words, we find a tool we can harness from within ourselves to confront the challenges and obstacles in our lives – Courage.

In Alcoholics Anonymous, there's what is known as the Serenity Prayer: "God, grant me the serenity to accept the things I cannot change; The courage to change the things I can, And the wisdom to know the difference."

Sometimes, and perhaps often, a part of Courage involves recognizing that the "Giant" lives within us, not outside in other people, situations, or events. In the encyclopedia of wisdom known as the Sunday Comics, do you remember Pogo the Opossum? He proclaimed, "We have met the enemy, and he is us."

Courage is the mental and emotional willingness to persevere in the face of fear. It's not the absence of fear. I once heard an interview with a professional race car driver who was asked if he was afraid when driving at 200 miles per hour. He said, "No, I'm not afraid. If I was afraid, I wouldn't be able to do it." What I learned was that driving a race car for a professional isn't a matter of courage; it's a matter of skill. So, we are wrong when we think of professional athletes, race car drivers, and daredevils as persons of courage. We would be much more informed when we think of people who go off to college, get married, and have children as acts of courage instead.

Consider courageous those who, when faced with daunting human and life struggles, carry on. There is much unhappiness in the world. Even the most well-adjusted among us still face tragedy. Life inevitably leads to death. The most blessed of us, who grow up with loving parents, maintain sound relationships, enjoy fulfilling careers, and form wholesome friendships, still face the death of our loved ones as our parents age or accidents strike. We may confront the destructive forces of violence, disease, or drugs as people we love are senselessly destroyed by forces that defy understanding and comprehension. In the stream bed lies a smooth stone, a stone with the power to stop a giant in his tracks – the stone of courage.

There is a movie entitled "The Bear." In it, a small bear cub (whose mother is killed by a hunter) is stalked by a Cougar and flees for its life, and escapes only to finally be trapped on a fallen tree across a stream. The Cougar creeps menacingly forward and the little cub trembles like Saul's soldiers and with its back against the stream turns and faces the Cougar. The little bear rises up on its hind legs and emits a pitiful growl. Suddenly, the Cougar stops in its tracks apparently startled by the Cub's willingness to fight, and begins to back up from the Cub. Then, the camera pans around in a circle revealing behind the little cub a huge Grizzly bear risen to full height on its hind legs glaring, snarling at the Cougar. We now understand the Cougar's fear, don't we? Yet, we might miss another point. The cub turned, it rose up on its feet, and it was prepared to fight. That is Courage.

Gratitude

The Fourth Stone is Gratitude. We were visiting with a friend, an old friend, of 50 years. We are old men now, and like old men, we were reflecting together, and somehow a question came up between us. "If you had to pick one word to describe your life, what would it be?" My friend said, "I think I would pick 'Gratitude.'" Sort of stunned, I said, "That is my very word." Part of what I share with that old friend is that neither of our early lives were particularly blessed. My family history is one of broken marriages, alcoholism, violence, and meanness, and his is not too very different. Both of us, somewhere along the line, found our footing, created a purpose, made a turn, and with the help of so many, did find a way to live a decent and even rewarding life. I was reading a book the other day and came across a little passage where the author wrote, "Maybe all we can hope for is to muddle through and help each other as best we can." It's a simple philosophy but worthy of consideration, don't you think?

Like any youth, I think, I occasionally wandered from the straight and narrow, and another of my oldest friends was my co-conspirator in "crime." One of the differences between us was that he was caught, and I wasn't. In a sense, at least a part of my Gratitude is that when I reflect back on my long life, I look at the many times life has simply broken my way. When the waves struck the shore, the crashing destructive waters broke the other way and left me standing to carry on. I am not without some personal pride and give some credit to myself for making decisions to use the opportunities presented to me, but mainly I am grateful to the people in my life who helped me along the way. The "Self-Made" person is a myth. No one of us who has survived and prospered in this life has done it alone, without others. Now, of course, I am here, in this place and time, reasonably healthy, reasonably strong, reasonably financially able to live with comfort, blessed with my wife, our children, grandchildren even, and with my limited gifts gone further than I could have imagined as a child.

I have often thought that we have grown up believing the wrong things about change, accomplishment, and goals. We measure our success by how far we have to go rather than how far we have come. Perhaps, we can consider that our goals can be measured by progress, not perfection. It might be wise to take to heart the idea that some of our best lessons come from our past mistakes, and those errors in the past form the foundation for the wisdom of the future. After all, thorns sometimes have roses. Once, as a younger man, I played a game called Fast Pitch Softball. One of the most famous pitchers of the time was a man named Eddie Feigner. He toured with a team named the "King and his Court." He toured with a team comprised of a pitcher, a catcher, and a first baseman, and one infielder/outfielder. Feigner threw a softball so fast that a batter had less than an eye blink to swing. I was selected to an "all-star" team to play against him. He, of course, threw one strikeout after another, and no member of our team even touched the ball until in one of the last innings I came up and bravely swung the bat. Amazing, I connected and drove the ball deep toward left field. Their utility player with lightning speed took off to chase down the ball as I ran to first and toward second as my ball curved down the left field line and out of bounds... a foul ball.

I returned to the plate and like my teammates then struck out. After the game, shaking hands with the opposing team, their first baseman said, "That's the best contact we've seen off Feigner in a long time." It was the best strikeout of the night! I remember that failure with Gratitude. Now, let's consider a bit here. This may seem trivial. And in one sense it is, and in another, it's the little things that count. If we can be grateful for the little things, then it can follow that we will be grateful for our larger gifts.

Justice

Now, we reach into our toolbox and take out our last stone, Justice. We began with Love and end here with Justice because, as Cornell West has told us, "Justice is what Love looks like in public." "Let your heart feel for the affliction and distress in everyone," said George Washington.

The arc of history bends toward justice, and it is our Biblical hope that Justice rolls down like waters. In its simplest and even purest form, Justice is the idea that others have the right to the same privileges that we have. Sometimes we get confused, and in our political world, Justice is supplanted by "Fairness," but they have different philosophical, ethical, and spiritual meanings. (More on this in Chapter 20).

What does it mean to be fair? Let's bring into play a couple of other words that sometimes substitute for Fairness – Sameness and Equality. Many might argue that we are fair when we are not biased and show no favoritism. "I treat everybody the same" might be an argument against helping. They would argue that the Declaration of Independence says that very thing, "That all men are created equal," and it follows that any laws, quotas, or special treatment even to address past ills are wrong because it isn't fair. It is not fair in the sense that it treats some people differently than others.

So then, what's wrong with this argument that all people should be treated the same and that all men are created equal? After all, that is what it says in the Declaration.

Well, one reason is that the Founders didn't set out to form a nation based on Fairness. They set out to build one based on Justice. A foundational principle of Justice is that "Equals should be treated as equals and unequals unequally." There is nothing quite so unequal as the equal treatment of unequals. Thus, the problem is that being "fair" always favors the privileged. In any race with predetermined starting and finish lines, the speedy will predictably win. Tax equally, and the poor suffer, and the rich gain. Treat children as adults, and you have a formula for abuse.

A Just Society takes into consideration that Need, Desert (as in deserving), Contribution, and Effort all come into play when considering how individuals are treated. So in America, we hold as an ideal, we know, we know in the sense that it is our national obligation, constitutionally defined, that children are not adults, that class does not entitle one to more than one vote, that education is the right of all, and that the general welfare is a more potent value than individual privilege.

So here we are at the end, thinking about life, thinking about obstacles, challenges, and life's struggles, and considering a small toolbox containing Courage, Gratitude, and Hope, bound together by Love and Justice. We have entered into a social contract that strives to ensure that we all share a co-equal right to live and prosper and that everyone has the right to the same privileges that I have.

The Book of Micah in the Old Testament tells us: (Micah 6:8) "He has showed you... what is good. And what does the LORD require of you? To act justly and to love mercy and to walk humbly with your God." And in the New Testament in the Book of Matthew (Matthew 22:37-40) when Jesus is asked what is the greatest Commandment, he replies: "Love the Lord your God with all your heart and with all your soul and with all your mind." This is the first and greatest commandment. And the second is like it: 'Love your neighbor as yourself.'

Whether one subscribes to the writing in the Judeo-Christian Holy book, the wisdom remains to "Act Justly" and "Love one another," with Courage, Hope, and Gratitude. I'm thinking about another otherworldly message brought to earth by a friendly alien. You remember him. His name was "Spock." He was a space voyager and explorer who, when he said goodbye, always left with a wish. He would say, "Live Long and Prosper."

12
ENLIGHTENMENT

A leaf falls in a lonely forest

A grey wolf howls in a barren field

An eagle flies over a rocky crag

A wood chuck digs in an empty hole

A reader turns the page of a book

Enlightenment finds but one

Thorns Have Roses

13
THE SECRET TO A BETTER WORLD

I am going to share a secret with you. Some may think it naive, maudlin, overly simplistic, or trite. Yet, I think if you were to follow this secret, your life, and mine, would be happier, more fulfilling, more satisfying and you would be thought of with praise and satisfaction. The secret came to me years ago when I was hiking in the Colorado Rockies. I was following another hiker some 50 yards or so in front of me. I saw him glance down beside the trail but then continue on his walk. After about 10 yards, he stopped, turned around, and came back to where he had glanced at the ground. He bent over and picked up a discarded soda or beer can, shook it free of water and dirt, and put it in his backpack. His action gave me pause. I thought about what he had done. In fact, I thought about it a lot. He could have continued on his way and I would have thought nothing of it. Yet, stopping, returning, picking up the discarded can, and putting it in his backpack, signaling his intention of putting it in the trash, all flew in the face of typical behavior. Most of us would simply have walked past (perhaps, with a condemning thought about the thoughtless and anti-environmental behavior of careless hikers) without giving it much thought ourselves.

Out of this seemingly small gesture, over time a world-changing idea came to me. Of course, this idea is not exclusive to me. Witness John Wesley's beautiful call to do good. "Do all the good you can, By all the means you can, In all the ways you can, In all the places you can, At all the times you can, To all the people you can, As long as ever you can." In fact, I have come to see it as the secret to a better world. It comes in two parts. First, think about that unknown hiker. What did he do? First, he picked up after some careless hiker. And second, when you think about it, the Park Service clearly knows about the sloppy, careless behavior of park visitors and employs workers to clean up the trails periodically. So the thoughtful hiker, in a single act, corrected the carelessness of one person and made the job of another much easier. So where does all of this take us? It takes us to the first part of the secret to a better world. It leads, in fact, to a simple, easy-to-do, no costs act that results in a cleaner, nicer, less expensive, and better world. This is the single one thing you can do that would make a better world. **Do More than Your Share**. Back to the thoughtful hiker for a moment. What did it take to pick up the can in time and effort? Mere seconds. What was the impact? A cleaner world, a more pleasant experience for other hikers; and, I suspect, some sense of personal worth. Oh, let us not forget the economic impact. The costs to the budget of the Park Service are reduced. Here's a fact. It is estimated that there are about 100 million pounds of waste is generated annually from park operations and visitors. Leftover food waste accounts for about 40%; paper and cardboard equals 22%; about 17% are plastics; glass accounts for roughly 7%; and reusable or recyclable stuff like camping equipment, fuel cylinders, food packaging, and propane cylinders are abandoned according to the National Parks Conservation Association. Now, I don't want to mislead you. The National

Park Service is struggling to cope with the rising amount of trash, but other private agencies and even corporate entities are working to deal with the issue, such as the National Park Foundation and companies such as Subaru and Tupperware. That's good, but think about this. Our national parks have more than 300 million visits a year. Apparently, every third visitor is leaving behind a pound of trash. Instead, what if every third visitor was like our anonymous hiker and "took only photographs and left only footprints."

"Doing more than your share" has more to do with our lives than public accommodations alone. I'm reminded of a story I read or saw on local television. It was about a man who lived in what we might call a lower socioeconomic neighborhood. He had noticed that his block was increasingly littered with trash – discarded cans, bottles, fast food containers, and the like. He began by cleaning up the sidewalk and gutter in front of his house. His neighbor was an elderly woman and he decided to clean up her sidewalk and gutter as well. Over time, he expanded to include the entire block. Obviously, doing more than his share. Neighbors noticed and some began to come out on Saturday mornings to chat with him and join in the neighborhood cleanup. It became a regular and continuing part of that neighborhood's care and maintenance of itself. One person's action led to a better, cleaner, more socially connected neighborhood.

My wife, Marie, takes a walk around our neighborhood daily. As she walks, she finds an occasional discarded item like a can or a candy wrapper, and she picks it up. As she passes the recycling container, she will drop off the plastic bottles or aluminum cans. A visitor to any grocery will often find a can or a package of chips that has fallen from the shelf. Customer after customer will walk past, waiting for a store employee to place it back on the shelf.

I read a book entitled "Nickel and Dimed: On (Not) Getting By in America" by Barbara Ehrenreich, in which she chronicled her attempt to live off minimum wage for a year. One of the chapters dealt with her employment at Walmart, where her job was to replace on the shelves articles returned or misplaced by customers. That was her job. Now, what would be the impact if, as a customer, you happened to walk down the aisles where Potato Chips were shelved and you saw a package of chips on the floor, and rather than walk past, you reached down and replaced it on the shelf? It is a small act, of course, and a single act would not have much of an impact. On the other hand, it costs you little in terms of time or effort. Yet, like the hiker picking up a can in a national park the impact of thousands of people doing more than their share would result in a less expensive trip to the grocery store. Everywhere we look there are opportunities to do more than our share that would make our world a better place.

I wonder how often each of us has heard the phrase, "It's not my job." Sometimes in our work life, we come across thoughtless, inconsiderate, even cruel decisions which upon consideration, leave us dumbfounded over how such decisions came to be made. I spent my life in academia and even though the people who worked there are among the most educated people in the world such small cruelties can occur.

I came across one of these. A faculty member's department was eliminated, but she was a tenured faculty member who was retained and assigned a new office on the floor of another department. The mailboxes for that department were housed in the department office and the department chair made the decision to have that unattached faculty member's mail placed on a chair outside the department office where she could collect it daily. Time passed, and as it happened, a new department chair was hired. After a short time, the new chair noticed the chair in the hall with mail and asked the department secretary what the chair was for. She told him the story and he instructed her to make a mailbox in the office and inform that unattached faculty member that in the future she could collect her mail in the office. After a few days, she came to the new Chair's office to thank him for the courtesy and consideration. Through tears, she told him of the humiliation she had experienced picking up her mail from the chair in the hall. The new Chair's job description didn't include showing a random act of kindness to a person not assigned to his department. In fact, it is an act of correcting the thoughtlessness of another. Such random acts of kindness are exactly what comes from doing more than your share.

I think there must be incalculable numbers of ways in which we could do more than our share and make the world, our neighborhood, our workplace, our relationships, and our very lives better by doing more than our share. Dry an extra dish, pick up a discarded candy wrapper, return a grocery cart to the store, let a car into traffic, drop a delivered package onto a colleague's desk, clean up the alley behind your house, pick up around the trash receptacle at the city park are all small ways each of us can make the world a better place. All of that is one part of the secret to a better world. As you do that, you become a gift to humanity.

As I look at the examples above, I am struck by how simple they are. Certainly, sophisticated and urbane readers might even consider them too simplistic and naive. How can we change the world by picking up a Tootsie Roll wrapper? Yet, reviewing the world's great religions and many self-help philosophies one finds the teachings of Jesus including the Sermon on the Mount, Buddha's Eight Fold Path, the Principles of the Boy Scouts, Alcoholics Anonymous, and other such teachings which all point to the importance of taking care of one another.

As I thought about that conscientious hiker picking up the discarded can I took notice of a second truth to contribute to a better world. He didn't immediately pick up the can. He at first passed it by. Then, he turned and returned to pick up the can. He paused, he reflected, and he made a decision. He made a decision to do the right thing.

When is the right time to do the right thing? This thought has occurred to many people and it is an often stated moral principle. **It is never too late to do the right thing**. Had the hiker returned the next day to pick it up it would still have been the right thing to do and would have still been doing more than his share and would have still contributed to making the park a better place to be a part of nature and would have still made the world a better place. No less a personage than Nelson Mandela said exactly that: "It's never too late to do the right thing." Martin Luther King Jr. said it this way: "The time is always right to do what is right." That is the advice in the 12 Steps of Alcoholics Anonymous. Step 9 reads: "Made direct amends to such people wherever possible, except when to do so would injure them or others," and Step 10 advises us, "Continue to take personal inventory and when we were wrong promptly admit it." In this sense, time is a gift. The past is the past and cannot be changed. But, in the present, we can make amends and in so doing clear the way toward the future. Doing the right thing, even at a late date, means we do not have to live with regret. Psychologists tell us that the best predictor of behavior is past behavior. The best predictor of what you will do now is what you did the last time. Our hiker is more likely to pick up a piece of trash the next time he sees it because he picked up the trash the last time. When can you change your behavior? It is the next time you have the opportunity to act differently.

So, Dear Reader, you and I have at our fingertips the secret to a better world. Pick up a discarded soda can or a candy wrapper, sweep the sidewalk or clean up the gutter not only in front of your place but maybe a bit over into your neighbor's place as well. Commit a random act of kindness, make room for another car in traffic, and, honestly, the world will be a better place. It doesn't take much, just a little, and, in truth, think of this . . . if each of us does more than our share, we will be happier, more fulfilled, and have a sense of meaning because we all will be living in a cleaner, healthier, kinder, and less expensive world.

See you at the trash can, my friends, when we have a chance to meet to drop off a found and discarded can!

Thorns Have Roses

14
TWO DUCKS — A PARABLE

There is the story of a man who went to an art show sponsored by an elementary school. As he entered the exhibit area, his eye was immediately drawn to a pencil and watercolor painting displayed on a far wall. Even from afar, it had a kind of aesthetic appeal that seemed to draw him toward it. It was not so much a real painting as it was two shapes rising out of the bottom of the paper. "Technically," it wasn't a fine painting, but it revealed the creative insight of a young mind seeing the feeling of a thing rather than the thing itself. He glanced at a neatly typed title, "Swans at Sunset." He then noticed that the label on which the title was typed was a little loose. He was an incurable loose-lable-looker-underer. There, under the label, written in the hand of some young artist, was the title of the painting, "Two Ducks."

Then there is the story of the art teacher who didn't know anything about art but thought he knew what people liked. But then, that is the same story.

*Originally published by I. D. Welch and E. W. Flink. (1980, Summer). Celebrations, 9. Reprinted by permission of the author.

15
THE LION WHO THOUGHT HE WAS A SHEEP

Once upon a time, a little lion cub wandered away from his mother and all the other lions in its Pride (the collective noun for a group of lions). Soon he was lost. When he started to look for his mother, he couldn't find her anywhere. He looked everywhere and all he could find was a flock of sheep. He was very little, even tiny, and really had no idea of who he was or for that matter what he was. He didn't realize he was a lion and since he didn't know what he was and he had never seen himself, he thought he must be one of those. So he became the lion who thought he was a sheep. And since he was so little, the sheep had no fear of him and just let him mingle right in with the flock. As he grew, he learned all the things that any sheep learns. He learned to eat grass (although to be truthful, he never really liked it). He learned to jump over rocks and he tried to learn how to sound like a sheep, but he never got his "Baaaaa" down quite right. He even learned to be herded around by the friendly old sheepdog. One day, as he was eating some clover (which didn't taste half bad), he saw the most beautiful creature he had ever seen. It was big and golden and glistened in the sun. As he watched, it lifted its mighty head and roared. As he listened the lion who thought he was a sheep, felt a strange stirring in his throat. His whole body shook with memory and a roar escaped from him that frightened and scattered all the sheep. From that day on, he was never a sheep again.

Moral: Sometimes it takes a lifetime to find out who we really are.

*Originally published by I. D. Welch and E. W. Flink. (1980, Summer). "The Changing Self: Two Stories. <u>Celebrations</u>, 9. Reprinted by permission of the author.

16
THE PIG WHO THOUGHT HE WAS A DOG

Once upon a time, there was a pig who thought he was a dog. His master taught him to roll over, sit, lie down, fetch, and speak. One day, while he was out hunting rabbits, he came across a group of pigs and they greeted him. "Hello, fellow pig," they said. "I'm not a pig," he replied. "I'm a dog." "A dog," they laughed. "you're not a dog. You're a pig just like us. Look at your snout. Look at your pointed ears. Look at your little beady eyes. Look at your curly tail. And just look at your feet!"

The pig who thought he was a dog looked at all those things and said, "I'm not a pig. I'm a dog. Look. I can roll over." And he did. "Look, I can sit up." And he did. "And I can bark." "Oink.," he barked. And with that, he went home, carried his master's slippers to him, and nestled at his feet. "And," he thought contently, "I can fetch."

Moral: Sometimes, in this modern world, even facts and objective evidence can't change the minds of some people. Their minds are set.

*Originally published by I. D. Welch and E. W. Flink. (1980, Summer). "The Changing Self: Two Stories. <u>Celebrations</u>, 9. Reprinted by permission of the author.

17
A SPECIAL CHAPTER FOR TEACHERS

Some years ago, The Colorado Association for School Counselors sponsored a contest for an inspirational essay or poem for their membership. I entered and won 1st Place with a poem/essay entitled "I Envision a Day." I read back over it recently and thought the sentiment was still appropriate and so I offer it here as a gift to our present teachers.

I Envision A Day

I envision a day when all the teachers of this land will subscribe to and abide by an educational Hippocratic Oath that promises, "Above all, I will do no harm."

I envision a day when teachers will hold firm to the principle that no philosophy of education, no method of discipline, and no desire for subject mastery will ever be elevated over the value of a single child.

I envision a day when all will know that the school is a special place, and in this place, these honored ones will be protected and developed.

I envision a day when we will put away the instruments of pain.

I envision a day when the merchants of cruelty will be silenced and the silence will reverberate around the globe, shouting for all to hear, sometimes in awe and always in appreciation. "In America, in America, they do not hit their children."

I envision a day when teachers will simultaneously light up the dark places of our lives and, through their caring, warmth and love, heat the sure conviction of our own self-worth.

I envision a day when our children will no longer suffer the indignity of a grading system — assigned, like so many cabbages, some to the gourmet kitchen and some to the refuse heap.

Thorns Have Roses

I envision a day when it lies within human understanding that human beings are cut neither from sow's ears nor from silk. The human fabric is unique and within the individual weave that is each of us lies the finest any of us has ever done and the cruelest of any of us.

Therefore, let us educate for that which is beautiful and noble within each of us and let wither, from lack of attention that which is cruel and ignoble.

And so, we send them to you, you educators, in the hope that you will use your knowledge, skills, and talents to help build their minds, their bodies, and their morality so it may be said that when they leave you they will leave with the capacity

    to love

        and be loved

            to work

                and be fulfilled.

*Originally published by I. D. Welch (1989, Winter). Colorado Counselor. Reprinted by the permission of the author.

18
THE STORY OF US

I'm going to tell you a story. It is an amazing and fantastic story and one which, perhaps, you have never heard. What makes it all the better is that it is a story about us. By "us," I mean people. Anthropologists label people by the term "Homo." It is part of the biological ladder, which includes Kingdom, Phylum, Class, Order, Family, Genus, and Species. For us, our biological classification is:

    Kingdom: Animal

    Phylum: Chordates (we have a backbone)

    Class: Mammal (we have hair and milk glands)

    Order: Primate

    Family: Homonidae

    Genus: Homo

Species: Homo Sapiens

I bring this up because what is even more startling is that we are not the only "people" to have lived on Earth. Since we are part of the Species Homo, what distinguishes us is the particular form of "Homo" we are. We are, in fact, Homo Sapiens Sapiens. Homo Sapiens Sapiens is the term now applied to modern humans. More about this later. As I said, once we were not the only Species Homo on Earth. There were others. The Smithsonian National Museum of Natural History has named at least 21 species that are recognized by most scientists as human. But, I am getting ahead of the story.

If we start at the beginning of this story, then we have to go far back. I mean far, far back. So far back that it is a number that is hardly understandable. Back, back, back 13.75 billion years ago.* That's right, billion. It is an event Astrophysicists label "The Big Bang." They call it a "Bang" because they think of it as an explosion. Everything we know, everything that exists comes from "The Big Bang." Animal, Vegetable, Mineral. Time, Space, Distance. US! Everything in the universe is made of the same material that was created at that moment and has since continued to expand from its point of origin. What is that point of origin? Well, here's the thing. The Big Bang happened everywhere at the same time and in the same place – that is, all at once and everywhere at once. Matter and space and distance all happened at once. (*The information on the origin of the universe is mainly taken from the landmark book by Roger Briggs, "Journey to Civilization," Collins Foundation Press, 2013, along with other sources). Then, Space expanded, distance appeared and matter thinned out. The Big Bang happened right where we are just as much as anywhere. The question arises, of course, of what existed before the Big Bang. The answer is unsatisfying to some but it is this. We don't know and further, we never will. Our world, our universe, was created in such a universe-destroying, universe-creating moment of heat and energy that everything was erased and we began with a clean slate. We start from scratch. Why am I making such a big deal of the Big Bang? It is because we are all made of the same stuff. The universe is in us and we are the universe. The poem Desiderata reads,

"I am a child of the universe," and that is mostly true. In fact, we are the universe and the universe is us.

So the Big Bang happened 13.75 billion years ago and space happened and matter began to spread out. As it spread out, separate clumps began to form. The first stars came about 13.3 billion years ago. The Milky Way formed about 12.7 billion years ago. The Earth formed 4.5 billion years ago. A billion years later in a mixture of organic, water, chemical, and, perhaps, electrical matter, life began on Earth.

Now, we are going to move from billions of years to millions of years. From billions to millions. In that vast span of time, life evolved from a boiling soup to the first life forms. From about 240 to 65 million years ago, we had the Age of Dinosaurs. They had a 175 million-year reign on earth – a reign that ended with a geologic catastrophic event. A giant asteroid struck the earth with an enormous blast that destroyed a vast area, creating shock waves, tsunamis, and creating a layer of ash that covered the earth, resulting in the death of vegetation and disrupting the food chain until approximately 75-80 percent of the living creatures on earth went extinct. The reign of the dinosaurs came to an abrupt end. Why interject this? The end of the dinosaurs meant that the scurrying little mammals hiding amid and under the rocks could creep out and develop and evolve, which, in fact, made it possible for us, the Genus Homo, to evolve. So, about 2.5 million years ago, the first human-like creatures appeared. They began making tools. Something that had not happened before. This is the beginning of the Genus Homo, which is the lineage that eventually led to modern humans. Like the one we have already traveled, it is a long road. This early Genus was named Homo Hablis or "handyman." It appears that three changes occurred that propelled Homo forward: tool-making, meat-eating (sorry to my vegetarian friends), and rapid brain growth. The evolution of many species led to Homo Erectus and Homo Neanderthalensis. We have reached a dividing line between creatures that would be called ape-like and human-like. Everything before Erectus (Labeled Homo Egaster in Africa) was ape-like and everything after was human-like. By 250,000 years ago, these tool-making, two-legged, upright, and large-brained human-like beings spread out of Africa and eventually made their way through the Middle East into Europe and Asia. The climate had changed and the forest had given away to savannas where an upright posture, tool making, and a hairless skin had taken on survival meanings. The growing brain and its problem-solving intelligence added significantly to survival. Driven by these climatic factors, another species was developing – Homo Sapiens (Idaltu) or anatomically modern humans. All of this is happening in Africa. It is approximately 200,000 years ago and Homo Erectus and Homo Neanderthalensis have moved out of Africa. These modern humans are labeled Homo Sapiens Idaltu because they maintain some archaic features and their brains probably functioned at a primitive level compared to modern humans. This becomes important later on. Even given these primitive skills they were still a competitive species and made the first move out of Africa around 100,000 years ago. Two groups made the move. The northern route moved into present-day Israel but went no further north. A second migration took a southern route toward present-day India. The Neanderthals were mostly centered in Europe and Homo Erectus mostly in Asia. Now Homo Sapiens were positioned to populate the earth. Then, something went terribly wrong for these early homo sapiens. The earth was again ravaged by another geologic catastrophic event. This time, it was a volcanic eruption. Mt. Toba erupted about 73,500 years ago with such force that its ash covered much of the earth. The resultant effect was a 1000-year volcanic winter which continued to devastate the homo sapiens population. As a comparison, many will remember Mt. St. Helens in Washington State (USA). Mt. Toba's eruption deposited more than 12,000 times the amount of ash as spewed out of Mt. St. Helens. The effect was that the entire population of homo sapiens was nearly wiped out. The devastation was so great that only a few thousand members of the species homo sapiens survived. These were the ones who had remained in Africa or perhaps somehow managed to struggle their way back to Africa. The debris from Mt. Toba spread east in a roughly triangular shape which covered mostly the area inhabited by homo sapiens. The Neanderthals in Europe and Erectus in Asia were mostly spared the ash fall. It is estimated that only a few thousand homo sapiens survived the Mt. Toba eruption and these few thousand individuals are the ancestors of all humans living today.

They clung to life mostly along the eastern shore of Africa in groups of perhaps 20 to 50 individuals and no more than 100. They survived by hunting, gathering, and fishing while living along the shore where food was available.

As if the astrophysical and paleoanthropological story I have told above is not amazing enough, what follows is astounding. It is about 70,000 years ago now. The earth is recovering from a 6 to 8 year volcanic ice age followed by a 1000 year cooling period. The few thousand Homo Sapiens Idaltu individuals who had survived living in small groups along the eastern coast of Africa are beginning to emerge into a more hospitable world. Surviving these harsh conditions perhaps resulted in a sharper intelligence, the development of skills, and a growing ability to pass these survival skills along to their children. Although the Mt. Toba super eruption nearly wiped out the entire population of Homo Sapiens, those that survived were forced to cope with harsh conditions. The environmental conditions demanded a more sophisticated social organization, more effective hunting skills, and a closer bond between individuals and the group. By 60,000 years ago, the evidence shows that humans were living in a significantly different way. The surviving humans were now behaving in ways that humans had never acted before. A new and never-before-seen human had emerged from the awful devastation of Mt. Toba and its harsh aftermath. What began to appear would be what many have called "culture." Sophisticated tools, elaborate art, body decorations, and apparent self-awareness. The new human was named Homo Sapiens Sapiens (Wise Human). Homo Sapiens Idaltu were anatomically modern humans, but Homo Sapiens Sapiens were what has been labeled behaviorally modern humans. By now a whole new constellation of behaviors was emerging over the passage of time. These include spoken language, self-awareness, art and music, sophisticated problem-solving, a concept of time, and a concept of God or gods as seen in rituals. As respectfully as we can phrase it, we now know the age of God. God is 60,000 years old. The ability to cooperate, coordinate and plan developed. Homo Sapiens Sapiens move out of Africa to populate Europe and Asia and, ultimately, the whole world.

Homo Erectus, perhaps because of an inability to adapt to changing environmental conditions, become extinct. The Neanderthals in Europe seem to have stalled in development and their culture and way of life gradually declined. The last of the Neanderthals died out about 28,000 years ago in a small cave along the coast of Spain. Their reign on earth ended by the competition of modern humans and an inability to adapt. Some Neaderthal DNA may exist in modern humans. Some estimate about 5 percent of the present population may carry Neanderthal DNA. That is all that remains of this once-dominant species. After more than a million years, of the many species of the Genus Homo that have inhabited the earth, we are the last one remaining. A few thousand humans clinging to the eastern coast of Africa survived the devastating geologic catastrophic Mt. Toba eruption and evolved a powerful brain, developed a viable social culture, and inhabited the earth. By 14,000 years ago, humans had reached every land mass on Earth.

The Story of Us

Event	Years ago
Big Bang – The Beginning of Everything	13.75 Billion
Earth Formed	4.55 Billion
First Human-like Ancestors	2.5 Million
First Anatomically Modern Humans (Homo Sapiens Idaltu)	200 Thousand
First Species Homo leaves Africa	100 Thousand
Near Extinction of Homo Sapiens – Mt. Toba (Long Ice Age – Estimated 12,000 Homo Sapiens cling to the East Coast of Africa)	73,500 Thousand
Great Leap Forward (Dramatic Brain Growth) (Biologically and Behaviorally modern humans leave Africa)	60,000 Thousand
Homo Sapiens Sapiens move into Europe	40,000 Thousand

Thorns Have Roses

Last Neanderthals die out in Spain	28,000 Thousand
Humans Cover the Earth	14,000 Thousand
Civilization begins	5,000 Thousand years

By about 10,000 years ago, agriculture appeared and along with it, the development of power over nature and power over others. Aggression appears, and if there is a villain in the story of human evolution, it might well be agriculture. As crops are planted and warehouses are built to store grain, it becomes apparent who has more and who has less. The need arises to protect crops and storage as villages and, perhaps, towns grow up around the fields and people become less and less hunters and gathers and more and more farmers. Groups form to protect the crops and soon armies will appear to either steal someone else's crop or to protect one's own. Hunter-gatherers had little need nor little history of conflict with one another but agriculture changed that as people became more settled and felt the need to protect their now more settled homes. It is now about 5000 years ago and we have arrived at the edge of civilization. Written language is developed and we begin the journey of religion, science, technology; and having conquered the earth look to the stars to continue our long, long road of evolution.

What are we to learn from all of this? The Big Bang, the development of the stars and planets, the growth of biological organisms in the primordial sea, dinosaurs and mammals, and eventually us? Two physical and biological facts are revealed. First, everything that exists was exploded into being by the Big Bang. Everything is made up of the same stuff that came from the Big Bang. The atoms that make up my body are the same atoms that make up the structure of a tree or the lava bubbling up from the core of the earth. Everything that exists is made up of the same stuff. We are a part of the universe and the universe is a part of us. Second, every human being living today is the descendant of a few thousand survivors who lived through a cataclysm and by mutation or ever-sophisticated cultural change evolved into, frankly, us. One predominant lesson from all of this is that Race is a myth. The concept of race is irrelevant in the larger scheme of history. Whatever differences one person or another sees in us pales before our similarities and biological heritage. Of course, all of life is a process of individuation and the human strand is no different. From small bands where the experience of life is so similar, where one is in constant contact with one another, where the bonds are so close the similarities remain intact. With the expanding world, we individuate and create different cultures, different languages, different religions, and different traditions. We learn that we cannot be content. We are the last known survivors of Genus Homo, but our tenure on earth is not guaranteed. Evolution continues. The need to grow, adapt, and change remains as crucial to us now as it did when our ancestors faced a devastated earth and needed to hunt, gather, fish, create shelter, and protect one another so that all could survive. And yet, as any successful person has been told, "Don't forget where you come from." My own thought about this is that we can be proud of where we came from. We come from good stock. We come from brave, robust, creative, and intelligent ancestors. I do not know how far we will continue into the future. I do know how far I extend into the past. I go all the way back to the beginning . . . and so do you.

19
TRANSCENDENCE

Looking out my late afternoon window
I see the moon high in a sky streaked with clouds
children have been playing with chalk
drawing their imagination on a sidewalk
Looking deep into the darkening sky
I feel the images form in my memory
Taking shape and warming the very reaches of my soul
So many years decade upon decade
the moon's light cast a feeble shine
On those bright thoughts
transcending the surly bonds of age
And formed a circle of moonlight
That throws a light of hope
Into a dark world.

Thorns Have Roses

20
LIBERTY AND JUSTICE FOR ALL

I have traveled a good bit. As I drive, I tune into radio all across the country. As a consequence, I have had the occasion to listen to quite a lot of Talk Radio. After a time, it became clear that the Talk Radio Hosts across stations and across states all seemed to concentrate on the themes of Freedom and Fairness as opposed to Liberty and Justice. That puzzled me and it led me to some speculations and an investigation of the sacred documents of our republic: The Declaration of Independence and the Constitution and into some history of the thinking of our Founders. I might add a bit of caution here. I suspect that most readers would take a look at this chapter and conclude that it is about politics. I'm arguing, however, that that is not the case. It is rather a chapter on philosophy or a worldview.

It is trying to get at how people tend to view the world and then find the words and arguments that best fit their assumptions.

Let's take a look at the Pledge of Allegiance

I pledge allegiance to the flag

Of the United States of America

And to the Republic for which it stands

One nation, under God,

With liberty and Justice for all.

It does not read "Freedom and Fairness" but rather "Liberty and Justice." A bit more about this later and why it makes a difference. Now let's review the Declaration of Independence.

We hold these truths to be self-evident, that all men are created equal, that they are endowed by their Creator with certain unalienable Rights, and that among these are Life, Liberty, and the pursuit of Happiness.

The Declaration does not read "Freedom" but, again, "Liberty." Next, let's take a look at the Preamble to the Constitution of the United States of America.

We, the People of the United States, to form a more perfect Union, establish Justice, insure domestic tranquility, provide for the common defense, promote the general Welfare, and secure the Blessings of Liberty to ourselves and our Posterity, do ordain and establish this Constitution for the United States of America.

The framers of the Constitution were striving to write a document that would "secure . . . the Blessings of Liberty" not only for themselves but for all future generations. They did not write a document that was meant to secure "freedom." Again, more about this later and why it makes a difference.

Sons of Liberty

The Sons of Liberty was a loosely organized group of American colonists and had members in all 13 colonies. It was a secret society and it was unlikely that all of the members were even known to one another. It is unlikely, as well, that the Sons of Liberty were a formal organization with elected leaders and a membership list. It was an underground organization that used a "Liberty Pole" or "Liberty Tree" to announce public meetings. They were the origin of the famous motto "No Taxation without representation." Some members who have come down to us through history were Samuel Adams, Benedict Arnold, Benjamin Rush, John Hancock, Patrick Henry, Paul Revere, and notably, Joseph Allicock, an African-American who was a leader of the Sons in New York. They were the "Sons of Liberty" and not the "Sons of Freedom."

Patrick Henry

There is a speech delivered nearly 250 years ago that is said to have convinced the Virginia delegation to the convention to commit Virginian troops for the Revolutionary War. In that speech, Patrick Henry entreated the Delegates to "Give me Liberty or Give me Death."

Abraham Lincoln – Gettysburg Address

Four score and seven years ago our fathers brought forth on this continent, a new nation, conceived in Liberty, and dedicated to the proposition that all men are created equal.

So now we have reviewed the Declaration of Independence, The Constitution of the United States, The Gettysburg Address and we have looked at the name the Colonists rebels gave to themselves and some of the statements of early patriots examining what they were fighting for. It emerges clearly that their revolution was one of seeking Liberty and not a revolution for Freedom. Finally, we have the Liberty Bell, Liberty Bonds, the Statue of Liberty and Liberty was the dominating patriotic force in America for our first 150 years.

So out of all of this, here's a question – Why does the Pledge read – Liberty and Justice for all?

Why doesn't it read Freedom and Fairness? Why in the Declaration does it claim that self-evident truth is Liberty and not Freedom? Further in the Preamble to the Constitution why is its purpose to establish Justice and not Fairness? Or, to secure the blessings of Liberty and not the blessings of Freedom? Why did Patrick Henry not cry out "Give me Freedom . . ." rather than, "Give me Liberty . . ."? Finally, why did the Colonists choose to call themselves the Sons of Liberty and not the Sons of Freedom?

Here's a thought. In fact, two. First, our Founding Fathers, as we so often label them, were smart, well-read, thoughtful, and steeped in the Enlightenment philosophy of the day. Thomas Jefferson subscribed to the political ideals of a Social Contract expounded by Francis Bacon, Isaac Newton, and Voltaire. They knew their dictionary – what I'm trying to say here is that the words they used were used on purpose. Second, contrary to common opinion, Liberty and Freedom are not the same thing and Justice and Fairness are not either. Why do the Talk Radio Commentators from the conservative or right-wing end of the philosophical continuum tend to use the concepts of Freedom and Fairness rather than the more historically accurate concepts of Liberty and Justice? And a corresponding question – why do those from the opposite end of the continuum tend to use Liberty and Justice?

It's a little bit of a twisting trail --- but let's see if we can't get there.

Liberty and Freedom

Let's look at Liberty and Freedom first and why those labeled "Conservatives" would be drawn to one and those labeled "Liberals" to the other. I said that Liberty was the dominating patriotic force in America for our first 150 years. In the Iraq war, our French allies didn't support us and so we renamed "French Fries" as "Freedom Fries." But in WWI, sauerkraut was renamed "Liberty Cabbage" and the Dachshunds as "Liberty Dogs." I suspect that the description "Freedom Fries" was selected not only because of the changed political climate but because of the alliterative effect of the words (Freedom Fries). Because of the shifting political climate and the influence of conservative Talk Radio we might name "Liberty Bonds" as "Freedom Bonds," and a modern-day patriot might well rewrite the Pledge as "Freedom and Fairness for all." What's the difference? Freedom has a few definitions: the quality or state of being free, freedom from arbitrary or despotic control, and the power or right to act, speak or think as one wants. It is this last definition that touches most closely upon the difference in the meaning of the two words. Liberty is defined as the condition where individuals behave according to their will and govern themselves, taking responsibility for their actions and behaviors. Liberty is thus tied more closely with a governing structure with the corresponding understanding that rights are granted. Liberty is used in the context of a legal framework. Liberty implies a system of rules, a network of restraint and order.

Freedom, rather than Liberty, came to the fore in the Roosevelt years (1933-1945) as a part of the New Deal, his Four Freedoms (Freedom of Speech, Freedom of Religion, Freedom from Want, and Freedom from Fear). Conservatives began to claim the word, beginning in the Cold War, and it was expanded to include not only individual rights/freedoms but economic values such as Free Enterprise and Free Markets. Ronald Reagan, in his 2nd Inaugural Address, mentioned Freedom 14 Times and Liberty only once. But it had taken on a subtle difference; it now had a negative sense to it. It was the absence of constraints on markets and individual action. It was the right of any person to do what they wanted. Economic freedom meant deregulation, tax cuts, weakening of unions, and Talk Radio took up the cause and Freedom became the watchword of Anti-Government sentiment, an anti-civil rights movement reflected in the "Right" not to deliver goods and services to people you disapprove of or who "offend" your sense of right or morality. Freedom propelled us into the Age of Entitlement and led to the "Me" Generation. The Logical, although extreme, endpoint of Freedom is Anarchy – with an anti-government step along the way – so strong a sentiment of the right end of the continuum today.

Liberals tended to focus on Constitutional Rights. Those rights granted by law, due process, and the right of petition rather than direct civil disobedience, such as we see in 2nd Amendment Protests, Tax Protests, or in the extreme actions of those who attacked the Capitol on January 6, 2021, where some small group declares that they are free to ignore laws and act because of their personal beliefs. Gradually in the shifting patriotic climate, Freedom, the power or right to act, speak, or think as one wants without any sense of governmental control or obligation has become the driving patriotic force of the Conservative Right.

It seems that thinkers from the left or liberal end of the continuum tend to focus on Liberty which implies a commitment to a group with a legal basis honoring a social contract (an example would be the ACLU or the American Civil Liberties Union. This is a group dedicated to protecting the "Liberties" granted in the Constitution) and seems to be more in line with the thinking of the Founders while Conservatives, at least the ones on the Far Right, seem to embrace the idea of the Rugged Individualist and the notion of a Wild West America where it's every man or woman for him- or herself society be damned.

Now, let's tackle the issue of Justice versus Fairness. Justice and Fairness are not only words with different meanings but different philosophical ends. Let's set the table. We are Americans and we have a deal with one another, a social contract. It's called the Constitution and here's the preamble again.

We the People of the United States, in order to form a more perfect Union, establish Justice, ensure domestic tranquility, provide for the common defense, promote the general Welfare, and secure the Blessings of Liberty to ourselves and our Posterity, do ordain and establish this Constitution for the United States of America.

Two important phrases for us here in this particular discussion. "Establish Justice" and "Promote the General Welfare." That's just setting the table. More about that in just a bit and why conservative right-wing talk radio and the general shift is toward Fairness and away from Justice.

What does it mean to be fair? Let's bring into play a couple of other words that sometimes substitute for Fairness: Sameness and Equality. Conservatives argue against Affirmative Action or admission standards that consider race because they say it isn't fair and that everyone should be treated equally or treated the same. In fact, the Right argues that we are fair when we are not biased and show no favoritism. "Fair" in this sense means not impartial or not showing favoritism. They would argue that the Declaration of Independence says that very thing, "That all men are created equal," and it follows that any laws or quotas or special treatment even to address past wrongs is wrong because it isn't fair – not fair in the sense that it treats some people different than others. We can be drawn into that argument because it seems like what we do believe. What's wrong with this argument is that all people should be treated the same and that all people are created equal – after all that is what it says in the Declaration. One reason is that the Founders didn't set out to form a nation based on Fairness. They set out one based on Justice and now we come face-to-face with a fundamental difference between the two concepts. A foundational principle of Justice is that "Equals should be treated as equals and unequals unequally." It's going to start getting a bit complex here because that means that all justice is not fair and all that is fair is not just. Conservatives, especially of the Libertarian camp, are really unhappy with this idea and argue instead that justice is merely about protecting property rights and the freedom of the individual. They do not have much sympathy for an overriding social contract that binds a society together in a commitment to protect the rights and welfare of the weak.

However, if we establish that society has a duty to treat people in a certain way, it is no use arguing that this responsibility is somehow subordinate to claims of fairness. And that is just what the Founders did in the Preamble.

We the People of the United States, in Order to form a more perfect Union, **establish Justice***, insure domestic tranquility, provide for the common defense, promote the general Welfare, and secure the Blessings of Liberty to ourselves and our Posterity, do ordain and establish this Constitution for the United States of America.*

Interestingly, some conservative Justices on the Supreme Court of the United States do not believe that the Preamble to the Constitution carries the weight of the other articles. They have argued it doesn't have anything to do with the intent or design of the Constitution. It's just an introduction.

The Founders, however, did take the path of a moral obligation that Society should follow the principles of Justice, not of fairness, that society must adhere to because justice is about doing what is morally required. Justice argues that all people are equal under the law, while Fairness argues that all people are equal and because it insists that all people are equal, then humanity becomes a vast, faceless lump. But a Just Society takes into consideration that Need, Desert (as in deserving), Contribution, and Effort all come into play when considering how individuals are treated. So, in the

United States, we know that it is our national obligation, constitutionally defined, that children are not adults, that class does not entitle one to more than one vote, that education is the right of all, and that the general welfare is a more potent value than individual privilege.

What continues to divide us are old, old issues in our understanding of our relationship with others: Civil (people) rights versus property rights, a Social Contract versus individualism, and continually wrestling with the definition and meaning of words such as Liberty and Justice against Freedom and Fairness.

As a nation, we are approaching a 250-year history. We are still struggling to decide who we are. Are we one nation with a population of 330 million or are we a nation with 330 million individuals. Those 330 million search around and find millions of others who mostly agree with them and then pit themselves against some millions of others who mostly disagree with them and set out to force control over them. Is that who we are? Or, are we the People of the United States trying to form a more perfect Union, establish Justice, seek domestic tranquility, provide national defense, promote the welfare of all, and secure the Blessings of Liberty for ourselves and for our children and even unto our children's children as were the ones who sacrificed their "lives, their fortunes, and their sacred honor?"

Thorns Have Roses

21
STATISTICS AND GRATITUDE

I came across the Statistics below from the internet. It reminded me again to find gratitude in life. Some of the many things we take for granted lie outside the lives of many people in the world. If you live in the United States of America, have a phone, eat regularly, have clean water, have access to the internet, and have a safe home, then you are among the privileged of the world. Add to the gifts above, having a college degree and living beyond 65 years, then you have prospered beyond 93% of the other people in the world. You are among the already blessed.

The population of Earth is around 8 billion. For most people, it is a large figure; however, if you condensed 8 billion into 100 persons and then into various percentage statistics, the resulting analysis is relatively much easier to comprehend.

Out of 100:

11 are in Europe

5 are in North America

9 are in South America

15 are in Africa

60 are in Asia.

49 live in the countryside

51 live in cities.

75 have mobile phones

25 do not.

30 have internet access

70 do not have the availability to go online

7 received a university education

93 did not attend college

83 can read

17 are illiterate.

33 are Christians

22 are Muslims

14 are Hindus

7 are Buddhists

12 are other religions

12 have no religious beliefs.

26 live less than 14 years

66 died between 15 – 64 years of age

8 are over 65 years old.

If you have your own home

Eat full meals and drink clean water

Have a mobile phone,

Can surf the internet and

have gone to college

You are in the minuscule privileged lot. (in the less than 7% category).

Among 100 persons in the world, only 8 live to or exceed the age of 65.

If you are over 65 years old, be content and grateful. Cherish life, grasp the moment. Take good care of your own health. Cherish every remaining moment.

22
WITH MIRTH AND LAUGHTER

I happened to see a story the other day. In a convent, the 98-year-old Mother Superior lay dying. The nuns gathered around her bed, trying to make her last journey comfortable. They tried giving her warm milk to drink but she refused it. One of the nuns took the glass back to the kitchen. Remembering a bottle of Irish Whiskey, she opened it and poured a generous amount into the warm milk. Back at Mother Superior's bed, they held the glass to her lips. The frail nun took a sip, then another and then a little more and before they knew it, she had finished the whole glass. As her eyes brightened, the nuns thought it would be a good opportunity to have one last talk with their spiritual leader. "Mother," the nuns asked earnestly. "Please give us some of your wisdom before you leave us." Mother Superior raised herself up in the bed on one elbow, looked at them, and said, "Don't sell that cow."

Now we live in troubled times that might require a wee sip to get through them. Times that might require us to face them With Mirth and Laughter. These are disastrous times and I'm remembering that nearly every Hollywood disaster movie begins with the government ignoring a scientist. Sometimes it is a bit difficult to follow the instructions we have been given with certainty and faith. I saw one of the first news conferences where the government was telling us to avoid groups of more than 10 with 16 people on stage! We are staying home. We are Social Distancing. We are reorganizing 40 years of photographs and in the midst of all this, how can we stay sane, healthy, and happy? Remember Rapunzel? Rapunzel was quarantined and ended up meeting her future husband. So there is some room for positive thinking. Turns out there is plenty of advice. We will take a short stroll down the path of happiness, where lots of people know the way. We will visit the modem science of happiness and explore discoveries for a more joyful life. There is more information on happiness than ever. A Google search on the word "happiness" reveals 718,000,000 hits and a search on Amazon books reveals over 50,000 books on the subject. A new branch of psychology, Positive Psychology, is dedicated just to discovering what makes us happy and how we can be happier. As you can well imagine, with millions of websites and thousands of books, there are lots of recommendations, lots of advice, and lists of dispositions, traits, and behaviors on staying well, staying sane, and being happy. So what are we to do with the blahs, boredom, irritability, loneliness, cabin fever, and even sadness? Let's just dive in. Let's talk about us for a moment, people, and how we are. For all the mystery of why we act the way we do in all the studies of human behavior, it distills down to two major factors; attitudes and behavior. If social psychologists have proven anything during the last 30 years, they have shown that the actions we take leave a residue within us. Every time we act, we increase the chances of doing that same thing again. Most people accept that attitudes lead to behavior. While this is true to a certain extent (though less so than commonly supposed), it is also true that our attitudes follow our behavior. We are as likely to act ourselves into a new way of thinking as to think ourselves into a new way of acting. Here's some guidance from a poet.

My grandmother once gave me a tip:

In difficult times, you move forward in small steps.

Do what you have to do, but little by little.

Don't think about the future, or what may happen tomorrow.

Wash the dishes.

Remove the dust.

Write a letter.

Make a soup.

You see?

You are advancing step by step.

Take a step and stop.

Rest a little.

Praise yourself.

Take another step.

Then another.

You won't notice, but your steps will grow more and more.

And the time will come when you can think about the future without dread.

Thorns Have Roses

~Elena Mikhalkova

So what are the behaviors that will help us deal with this international mess? I'm re-reading "The Little Engine That Could" and even paying some attention to what the scientists recommend.

The Mayo Clinic tells us that laughter stimulates the body's organs increases oxygen intake, and triggers the release of Endorphins, what lots of folks call the "Runner's High." Science also tells us that laughter helps people handle stress, relaxes the muscles, and lowers blood pressure. Yep, apparently Hollywood and Tin Pan Alley had it right all along. There are plenty of old songs that encourage us to "put on a happy face," "smile when your heart is breaking," or "don't worry, be happy." I saw an action movie once where this actor was to star in a police drama and wanted to study a real police officer to be more realistic in the role. They got caught up in a really dangerous, violent confrontation with terrorists, and the actor was terrified – shaking in his boots. The heroic police tough guy says to the actor, "You're an actor, right?" The actor said, "Yes." The tough guy says, "Act brave." Kind of a funny story but then it turns out to be sound advice.

One way to confront isolation, sadness, loneliness, or even the simple blahs is to act happy. Whoa. Easy to say, right? Experts suggest imagining being with someone you love can be powerfully healing and soothing. Do a little experiment with me. Close your eyes for a moment. Now, imagine being with someone you love, someone who cares about you and who isn't here with you today. Now, imagine this person offering you a warm smile. Lock that image in place, take a deep breath and slowly open your eyes. Did you find you were smiling? Did you feel warmth around your heart ... like a hug, as you imagined that person? I hope so.

So right out of psychological research comes these recommendations. Be friendly. Friendliness is about offering warmth and good humor to those around you. As Human Beings, we are social creatures. In the grand history of things, it has been said that we have no reason for being here. We aren't the strongest creatures, the fastest, the most likely to survive. We are here because of our ability to cooperate and form social relationships aided by language and an opposable thumb. So every chance we get – Smile. There is a Zen koan or riddle, "Practice smiling while peeling carrots." It is just one of those things ... being able to offer a sunny disposition to the world, regardless of your inner state, actually encourages you to physically feel better. Smiles are contagious. We feel better when our smile is returned. A genuine smile has been found to be emotionally and mentally healing. One last thought on this idea. Years ago, during the Depression years, a famous American psychologist, George Kelly, was working at a small state college in Kansas, Ft. Hays State College (now Ft. Hays State University). Western Kansas then, as it remains now, is a rural area and the population is very dispersed. Kelly developed an innovative idea of a mobile psychological clinic and he traveled around the area and offered psychological counseling in rural communities. He could only visit occasionally, say every two months, so continuous therapy wasn't possible. Also, the farmers and ranchers of Western Kansas didn't take well to the dominant Freudian therapy of the era and so Kelly had to adapt. He developed a form of therapy loosely labeled "Fixed Role Therapy," in which he asked the client to play a role until he could return. If they were anxious they were asked to act confident. If they were depressed, they were asked to act happy. This, of course, was only until Kelly could return the next time and then they would take up therapy again. As it turned out, often these farmers reported they didn't need any further assistance from Kelly two months later since they were now acting in more confident or happier ways. So this advice, "Fake it 'Til You Make It!" has sound psychological backing. Gritting your teeth and bearing it is not the best option. Letting yourself smile during struggle is what brings a change in perception. So a straight-out, first order of business recommendation in these troubling times is to "take care of yourself." Among those trained in disasters, there is a saying - "Put the oxygen mask on yourself first." Because if we want to take care of others, then we have to first take care of ourselves. And following the advice of that well-known philosopher, Nike, "Just Do It."

Once, there was a farmer who grew award-winning corn. Nearly every year, he would enter his corn at the County Fair and win the gold medal. His corn was praised all around the state and a city journalist decided to interview the farmer. During the interview, the journalist learned that the farmer shared his award-winning corn seeds with all his neighbors. The journalist was a bit surprised and asked, "How is it that you share your seeds with your neighbors when they might end up competing with you at the Fair?" "Well," he said, "you know the wind picks up the pollen from the ripening corn and swirls it from field to field. If my neighbors grow inferior corn, then cross-pollination might degrade the quality of my corn, too. So, if I'm to grow great corn, then I have to help my neighbors grow great corn too."

So it is with our connections in life. If I want friendly neighbors, I need to be a friendly neighbor. If you want to be loved, learn to love others. Those who choose to be happy must let others find their happiness as the welfare of each is intertwined with the welfare of all. I remember a quote from Mary Church Terrell who founded the National Association of Colored Women (NACW) and was a founding member of the NAACP "Lift as you climb." So as we think of others, check up on your neighbors. Find out how they are doing. Put a note and a cookie in the mailbox for the letter carrier. Get out of the house if you can and wave at the neighbors. As Marie and I walk around our neighborhood and see a neighbor outside we will stop to talk. Sometimes another neighbor will come out and soon there will be a little neighborhood meeting - all practicing social distancing, of course. But also practicing social connectedness. Be compassionate. Sometimes in periods of stress, we can get cross-ways with our neighbors and even our friends. Be the one who seeks to mend the fence even when it was their cow that broke it down. When we accept others' shortcomings or cut others slack for their wrongs or missteps, we are valuing humanity over someone's flaws. Most of us are truly doing the best we can at any given moment. Sure, some days our "best" is far from "enough," and there are days when we know that we are guilty of giving less. No one is at 100 percent on their game every day. On his deathbed, Goethe, the German philosopher and poet, is supposed to have said, "Light. Light. The world needs more light." I think Goethe was wrong. He should have said, "Warmth. Warmth. The world needs more Warmth." Because we will not die from the darkness but from the cold.

If you accept the shortfalls of others, the windfall for you is a happier life. Gratitude is the quality that allows us to see the world as bigger than ourselves. As a part of that "Take Kindly the Counsel of the Years." We all know that growing old isn't for sissies and it can be a tough row to hoe sometimes. But we also know something else and that is – we have lived through a lot. We know that things pass. One of the reasons the teenage years are so tough is that those are the years when we are experiencing many things for the first time - we have no perspective - first kiss, first love, first betrayal, first meaningful success. We have no way of knowing that these painful or joyful experiences are the normal passing experiences of life and are not the sentences of a lifetime. Old age, if nothing else, gives us perspective. Just owning our good fortune, no matter how seemingly slight or minimal, can boost our overall well-being. Our level of gratitude is inversely proportional to our level of depressed feelings or sadness. In this hopeful equation, the more grateful you are in life, the better the chances are that you will enjoy what you have!

Look out the window and, if you are able, step out onto the deck or walk around the neighborhood. Marie and I dyed eggs at Easter, hid them, and had an Easter Egg hunt. Great fun! Consider visiting the senior recreational and communications center, watch some movies. Whoever knew that staying home, lying on the couch and watching TV would be our Civic duty! We can thank the pandemic for that. One unexpected, unusual, and positive outcome of this pandemic and stay-at-home social isolation is the discovery that the Earth is healing itself. Our air and our water are cleansing themselves as we have equilibrium. And so can we. There is hope that we can remember this time as a time when we found the "strength of spirit to shield [us] in sudden misfortune." Let a poet take us home.

> History will remember when the world stopped
> And the flights stayed on the ground.
> And the cars parked in the street.
> And the trains didn't run.
> History will remember when the schools closed
> And the children stayed indoors
> And the medical staff walked toward the fire

Thorns Have Roses

And they didn't run.

History will remember when the people sang

On their balconies, in Isolation

But so very much together

In courage and song.

History will remember when the people fought

For their old and their weak

Protected the vulnerable

By doing nothing at all.

History will remember when the virus left

And the houses opened

And the people came out

and hugged and kissed

And started again.

Kinder than before.

~**Donna Ashworth**

Thorns Have Roses

23
"CIVILIZATION AND ITS DISCONTENTS": INSTITUTIONAL OPPRESSION AND THE AUTHENTIC SOCIETY

The Impersonal Domain

We live our lives in a widening field of engagement. We evolve and develop an inner, personal psychic construction of the people, interactions, situations, and events of our lives. We develop strategies for interpersonal relationships. As we move out further in our involvements, we have to learn to deal with the groups and institutions of our society and world. This is the domain of impersonal relationships. Our institutions can be forces for good or ill in our lives. They can be the source of oppression and they can be the source of our liberation. If they teach a diminished philosophy of social responsibility, awareness, and involvement, then they are forces of oppression. If they seek to recognize privilege among only a few in society, then they are forces of oppression. If they diminish the worth of the individual against the corporate or governmental good, then they are forces of oppression.

If they seek to guarantee the rights of the weak from the strong, then they are forces for liberation. If they seek to provide fair and equitable treatment and concern for all, then they are forces of liberation. If they protect the individual against the power of the state, then they are forces for liberation.

This is a confusing area for many of us and one that can corrupt the morals and values of many. The subjugation of indigenous people all over the world, the horrors of World War II, the Stalin terrors, and the "killing fields" of Southeast Asia all point to the willingness of individual men and women to give up their values to do the will of the State. We have demonstrated ourselves willing to enslave, brutalize, and murder in the name of religious, national, and even financial institutions. This is the oppression not of single individuals but of entire peoples. Frighteningly, these mass horrors are not committed by monsters but by ordinary people "following orders." Such was the case in Nazi Germany and such is the case for all genocidal acts. Hannah Arendt, after her study of Adolph Eichmann, concluded that the face of evil was banal (in this sense "common" or "ordinary"). It reminds us again that social justice is the willingness to grant to others that which we wish for ourselves.

The great question of this domain is the struggle for autonomy and full citizenship. Somehow in the give-and-take of negotiations between institutional needs and individual worth, we seek a balance that permits the practice of social concern and social obligation alongside individual development and worth. Liberation argues that in these negotiations it is in the institutions of our lives that the give must take place. In weighing the rights of institutions and the rights of individuals, we give greater importance to the worth of the individual. If we could quote that great moral philosopher Arthur Fonzarelli (aka "The Fonz), "Hey, institutions aren't cool. People are cool." This is the difference between honoring an abstraction and honoring a corporeal reality. That is one of the great confusions. Institutions can invade our consciousness and leave us thinking that philosophy, governments, religion, or other abstractions somehow transcend the worth of people. This is a dangerous belief and one that Liberation thinking argues against.

In the struggle to understand our relationship with the groups and institutions of life, we have adopted many strategies. Those below reflect a way to understand the broad decisions each of us has to make as we seek an accommodation between our individual development and our social obligations.

What shall our relationship with institutions be? Shall we be dependent upon them to decide the great moral and values questions for us? Shall we independently make decisions about what is right and good for ourselves? Shall we find some way to balance the needs of the self with the needs of society? In the discussion below, we will look at the strategies of dependence, independence, and interdependence.

The Strategy of Dependence

Some have decided to become loyal subjects to a master. It might be a person or an ideal, a religious doctrine, or a political philosophy. They have given up their privilege and opted instead for the security of being a follower. Their legal, ethical, and moral decisions are dictated from outside the self and they are thus free of responsibility. It is an odd arrangement, isn't it? What shall it be? Enslaved and without responsibility or free and accountable and responsible. Erick Fromm addressed this issue in his work Escape from Freedom (1941) and I will return to it later on. Essentially, Fromm believed that freedom carries with it responsibilities and these create anxiety for us. Some find the anxiety to be intolerable and decide that security is more important than freedom. They become dependent rather than assume responsibility for their values and acts.

One of the old teachings in psychology is that "dependence creates hostility." It is this recognition that accounts for some of the tensions that exist in families as children approach maturity. Both parents and children are ambivalent about approaching independence. Children resent those times when they recognize that they are not fully independent (a goal that in itself has problems discussed below) and must rely on their parent(s). The parent(s) see the growing competence and striving for independence and fear for their child. While children are not the topic of this discussion and naturally need a state of dependency as they slowly develop toward maturity, the relationship between dependency and hostility that exists in families parallels those that exist in any relationship of dependency. The dependent party resents dependency even when it stems from a decision to give up autonomy. That is exactly the splinter that pricks at their conscience. They know, at some level, that they are not being true to themselves and their anger is displaced from themselves onto the master - institution, government, or religion. They are simultaneously obsequious and angry, fawning and discontent.

Dependence is a state that defies liberation. Dependence is a relationship of subordination and subservience. Liberation is a state of being in which one is simultaneously responsible for one's actions and not bound to any master. Obligations, commitments, contracts, and other agreements are all entered without duress and are respected. None of these concepts (commitment, contract, or even obligation) can exist in a dependent relationship. Why? Because these are concepts that require mutuality. A concept missing, of course, in any dependent relationship.

The Strategy of Independence

The alternative most often proposed to dependence is independence. While that view is widely held and often sought as a goal. It may well be a false goal and one as fraught with dangers as dependency. Like many others, however, independence can exist along a continuum in which relative independence and absolute independence have different meanings. What is wrong is the concept that human beings are isolated in the world and that we have to be wholly self-reliant. Self-reliance, as anything other than a relative concept and a temporary state, is an alien idea in human development and evolution. We are intrigued by the story of human accomplishment in which a single individual has triumphed against all odds in a struggle with nature or some other traumatic event. One of the most dramatic of these is the book *Mawson's Will* (1977) by Lennard Bickel. What is sometimes lost in stories of individual heroism (and make no mistake, Mawson is heroic in his struggle for survival) is that the goal of their survival is to reconnect with others. In the case of Mawson, an Antarctic explorer, he struggled to make his way back to a base camp where he needed the assistance of others. He is only alone and separate in his ordeal. He is not alone in the world. His ultimate survival is based upon his making it to human help. I mean by this that his independence is temporary and that his life, his ultimate survival hinges on the willingness and competence of others.

Thus, some would argue that independence is a myth. As a goal of life, it suffers from the problems of pursuing any myth. It is vaporous. Seemingly real, it fades as we seek to approach and disappears in the grasp.

We have many myths of independence that hamper us as we seek to understand our place in the world. The myth of the "rugged individualist" of the old west, the myth of self-made success, and the myth of self-reliance all influence our choices and decisions to some degree. Yet, each is false in some way.

The danger in striving for independence is the loss of community. We can see ourselves as an isolate and not a part of some larger whole. The danger is that as one comes to believe in an encapsulated self, there are no bonds connecting the person to society. The self can become alienated. This is one understanding of those who have become dangerous to society. They see no connection to themselves. Their victims are anonymous, unknown, and unconnected to them. Some say that the murder of a stranger, the murder of a convenience store clerk unknown and unprovoked, is a more dangerous crime than the murder of an acquaintance or family member. In the latter, motives can come to be understood. In the former, the brutality is "senseless" in that it has no personal motive behind it. It is violence for violence's sake alone. This is a greater danger because it signals indiscriminate violence and unpredictable harm. We are left with no protections in an unpredictable world.

This is, of course, a far reach from what most people mean when they say they want to be independent. What we mean when we use the word in this way is that we want to have a say, perhaps even the majority vote, in the decisions of our lives. We don't mean that we don't want to be in communion with our neighbors. We want to be connected, not separated, isolated, or disunited.

The Strategy of Interdependence

The strategy of liberation is the condition of interdependence. Life sometimes presents us with situations and circumstances in which it is necessary, even life-demanding, that we act autonomously. Sometimes, in values-challenging dilemmas, we might be called upon to stand alone. It is sometimes necessary and it is good to be able to act decisively and independently.

It is equally true that sometimes life asks us to act in concert with others to effectively reach a collective goal. Sometimes the tasks are too great for a single individual and, to be effective, we have to ask for and accept the aid of others. Sometimes the skills, competencies, and knowledge we need to reach a goal lie with another and we have to depend upon them to use their skills and knowledge in our cause.

All of this is true. A liberated person is one who sometimes acts independently and sometimes has to depend on others. It is a process of ongoing bargaining, compromise, and agreement. It is a process of fluctuating life circumstances, situations, events, and people that ebbs and flows sometimes in and out of our control. The liberated person can act independently when necessary and appropriate and can depend on others when needed and appropriate. Interdependence implies that one can be both a helpful friend and a grateful recipient of help. This is the path of liberation. To be an autonomous person, one does not have to be alienated, lonely, isolated, or oppositional. The autonomous one can both act independently and accept help when necessary. And, as the Serenity Prayer suggests, having the wisdom to tell the difference.

Thorns Have Roses

24
MOUNTAIN TOP

I take the far view

Things look small

I take the near view

Things look big

I take the inner view

Things look personal

I take the large view

I touch wisdom.

Thorns Have Roses

25
HOPE, OPTIMISM, AND THE FUTURE

I'm not a seer with special knowledge of the political, social, or economic future. I don't claim any special insight into the future. I do consider myself reasonably well-informed about the social and political issues of my time. As I consider the future, I wonder what sort of world the children of the present will inherit. The world I live in now was unimaginable in my youth. I am uncertain if those predicting the future so many years ago would have come anywhere close to the reality of the present. However accurate or imprecise our predictions may be, it is certainly necessary to plan for the future. The prediction comes with some cautions. If one checks back on how the futurists of the 1950s and 1960s imagined the 21st Century, one will find that they were overly optimistic. For example, the view was that by the year 2000, we would have a world of peace, prosperity, health, longer life, more leisure, and greater luxuries than ever known. A woman might be President. Viewing the national news through TV, social media, news magazines, or newspapers will dispel that optimistic prediction.

What cautions should we consider if we were to venture into the chancy world of predicting the future? One we have seen above. It is a sure mistake to assume that everything is going to turn out all right. That is the mistake of Optimism. Optimism assumes the future. It assumes that everything will work out all right in the end. There are, of course, arguments in favor of an optimistic point of view. Research into surgical outcomes shows that a positive view of the outcome by both the physician and the patient can result in a better outcome. Some sports psychologists insist that players with an optimistic view of their performance do better on the field. While these points of view deserve consideration, they do not seem to have parallels in the social and political world. Optimism throws a bias into our predictions. An overly optimistic view of the future can even operate to stall or prevent preparation and planning for negative outcomes. Such a bias can distort not only our predictions for a successful outcome but distort our view and understanding of present events. Let us use here the controversy over Climate Change and its causes, rate, and outcome. Some argued that the changes we were seeing were merely the natural climatic changes that have occurred throughout the centuries and that humans were contributing to the rate and severity of the change was somehow politically motivated.

Some argued that the data were false, manipulated or exaggerated. The impact was that the steps needed to slow or reverse climate change were resisted and delayed. It seems clear that a view of the future in which it is assumed that everything will be all right, that the steps we are taking are likely to be effective, and that there is no real need for concern over the future is ill-advised.

For all the dangers of an optimistic point of view in predicting the future, its opposite is more problematic. Pessimism reflects a point of view that tends to think that the worst aspects of a situation will ensue. It reflects a negative view of future events and reflects a lack of hope for the future as well. Pessimism sees the world as a place in which evil will ultimately overcome good. Again, sports psychologists would argue that a pessimistic point of view would actively interfere with a successful performance. Success is unlikely since the person wouldn't even attempt. Further, pessimism has shown itself to be associated with mental health issues including depression and stress. It has been linked to suicidal thoughts or ideas as well. The difficulty is that the person sees him- or herself as a passive agent in the world. They have little or no power to influence their lives or events. Any chance of success lies in the external world and outside factors that cannot be controlled. Essentially, a pessimist continually asks the question, "What's the point of trying?" Another unfortunate outcome of pessimistic thinking is that they have little faith, trust, or confidence in others. Closely related to pessimism is cynicism. Cynics, like pessimists, have little trust in others and view other's attempts at influencing events as naive, doomed to fail, or as only self-serving. In contrast to both optimism and pessimism, hope extends one's values into the future and contributes to success. Hope expresses our wishes for a sought-after outcome, a desire for a better future not only for ourselves but for others as well. Hope provides motivation and encourages effort and persistence. Yogi Berra reminds us that "it ain't over 'til it's over." Hope does not predict an outcome, it only reflects our desire. Hope expresses what our desired future is, but it doesn't guarantee the future.

The dictionary might suggest that "hope" and "optimism" are synonyms, and in common usage, that might be the case. But, the difference between the two words is in predicting the outcome. For an optimist, the outcome is positive and assured. In hopefulness, the outcome is unknown. In truth, the fact that the future is unknown is a cause for hope.

As I have said above, I have no more knowledge of the future than you. All I have written above is justification for my attempts below to see ahead and for how I look forward. I am most certainly not pessimistic about the future. Our whole history is one of struggling against forces, both natural and humanly created, to work toward a wholesome and humane world. I think that humans have within us the capacity to develop such a world. I am equally not optimistic about the future. We have many problems and issues which challenge us. It isn't clear to me that these problems and issues will be successfully addressed. For all of that, I am hopeful.

What does the future hold for us? I don't know. I do think there are challenges in the present that if we do not address them and do not resolve them humanely, darken our future. By humane, I mean a just, caring, and democratic one where everyone is considered to be of worth and can build their minds, their bodies, and their morality, so it may be said that all can love and be loved, work and be fulfilled. By democracy, I mean that every person is of equal worth and has a right to participate in the decisions which directly affect their lives.

There are, of course, many issues and problems which confront us in the present. There are four, however, which seem to me that must be confronted and solved in such a way that the democratic hope is fulfilled and provides for a more humane world. For me, these four are Extremism, Water, Climate Change, and Viruses.

Thorns Have Roses

Mass shootings are seemingly a daily occurrence. Shopping malls, schools, and the workplace have all been scenes of slaughter. The shooters are possessed of views and attitudes that dehumanize the victims and justify their murder. The views are so far from the mainstream of thought that our efforts to understand leave us dumbfounded. Who, outside adventure and espionage novelists, would ever think that the Capitol of the United States would come under violent attack by its citizens? When we seek to understand their thinking and motivation we are confronted with twisted reasoning of individual rights and freedoms and puzzling lines of authority justifying their treasonous actions. In my own life, I have lost friends, even close friends, whose political views have become so extreme that we no longer seem to have a common place from which to talk about political differences. I suppose you will have to take me at my word, but I am not a political radical. I see myself as mostly moderate in political concerns and admit that I lean strongly toward human rights and social justice issues. I have found that even though I consider myself a moderate, my thinking regarding human rights and social justice is seen in the eyes of some as "radical," and people like me are viewed with suspicion and even with malice. Long ago, when I was an undergraduate in college, I was the President of the Young Democrats. The President of the Young Republicans, at the time, and I would meet frequently in the Student Union for lunch and we, of course, argued over our differing opinions, over our views of government, and the solutions proposed to deal with local and national issues. We liked and respected one another. It never entered our minds that one or the other of us was un-American, immoral, unpatriotic, or corrupt. Somehow, in America, this has changed. I have my thoughts on this. It stems somewhat from the decision to end the Fairness Doctrine, resulting in the rise of Talk Radio, the proliferation of overwhelmingly conservative commentators, the dominance of Fox political commentary on Cable TV, and the resulting access to extremist positions which have always been underground in America but now have a voice. It further seems that the issue of Abortion once it was accepted as a political rather than a personal or medical issue, has separated us into irreconcilable opposites. My entire professional life has been spent in the world of education. It is a profession of ideas, information, data, and facts. It is a world of challenge. One idea may be pitted against another. Information is gathered. Arguments are presented. The facts are checked. A conclusion is reached. One of the valued outcomes of a college degree is supposedly the learned ability to tell a good idea from a bad one. The way to do that is to get information, consult authorities, and think it through. One of the mind-boggling modern political trends is the rejection of fact-checking, the condemnation of experts, the ridicule of higher education, and the refusal to check the origin and authenticity of information. Opinion has come to be more important than fact. This trend must be confronted. If it is not, it seems to me, the world will become a far more dangerous place than it is now. Even in the present, our schools, shopping centers, and places of employment can come under attack from extremist thinkers who have abandoned accepted ways of checking their violent thoughts. We have to find a way to make it clear that it is extremism itself which threatens our safety and our society.

The old west stank. That is to say, it was a foul, smelly place. One reason for that is that, relatively speaking, there was very little water. So what? The estimate is that the pioneers, cowboys, and other denizens of the old West didn't bathe very much. Say once a year. Once a year! Plus, the water of the old west tended to be brackish, polluted, and foul-tasting. Yep, those Western movies had it right. Cowboys drank a lot of whiskey. Since the water was unsafe to drink, they drank alcohol as a substitute. You might have heard of a place named Sweetwater. That's because the people of the West (Native Americans included) made a special note of places where the water wasn't brackish or salty. If you lived in a town, it was likely that water was hauled up from a nearby river or stream. Most towns dug a well, installed a windmill, and pumped the water through pipes to individual buildings. Sometimes that was an on-and-off proposition since the water table in the old west was often shallow. Water shortages were common. The water from these sources was often poor due to pollution due to unsanitary waste disposal, mining, cattle ranching, farming, and even industrial activities. The point of all this is that water was a problem in the old west and it continues to be a problem in the modern west. The modern West is drying up and as a consequence, water shortages are a present and future concern. Our two largest reservoirs are already dangerously low. These dangerously low water levels threaten our source of power and electricity, as well as the amount of water itself. As far back as 2018, I read an article advising smart investors to buy stock in water companies since water shortage in the future was going to create private entities to market water in the same way we market electricity or propane. Even at that writing, it was revealed that there was already a company in a major city that was selling memberships that permitted the members to access water fountains in downtown streets. Only those with membership numbers could drink from these fountains, creating a privileged class. The prediction was in the future that access to water would be controlled and available only through either private enterprise or publicly regulated companies. Now these years later, that prediction has yet to be proven. Yet, water shortages all over the nation are real and becoming more severe. It becomes one more of those problems which, if not addressed in the present, condemn the future.

I may have put the cart before the horse in discussing water. The issue of water shortages stems from the overall problem of climate change. Climate change (a bit more about this below) isn't a new issue for us. On a TV news program I saw recently, it was reported that as far back as 1912 concern was raised about burning fossil fuels and the effect it was having on climate. In modern times, a concentrated disinformation campaign has been waged, mostly by big oil companies, in which more than $100 million a year is spent on denying, discrediting, and misleading information on climate change. The U.S. House of Representatives Oversight Committee wrote to the chief executive of ExxonMobil that they were "concerned that to protect . . . profits; the industry has reportedly led a coordinated effort to spread disinformation to mislead the public and prevent crucial action to address climate change." BP, Chevron, Shell, ExxonMobil and the American Petroleum Institute have all resisted and blocked climate change initiatives. As one example of the impact of the campaign to stop, slow or distort informing the public of the dangers of the changing climate, the term used early in efforts to find methods to combat the use of fossil fuels and the impact of humans on the climate was "Global Warming." The disinformation campaign of big oil and others made such a mockery of "Global Warming" whenever a snowstorm hit or temperatures were below normal in some part of the country, or showed temperature changes throughout history to discredit the finding that climate changes were impacted by humans that the term was dropped in favor of "Climate Change." Whether the term is global warming or climate change, the earth is getting hotter. All over the world, people are experiencing heat waves and an increase in hot days. One of the hottest years on record was 2020 and in 2023, Death Valley recorded a temperature of 133 degrees. These hot temperatures contribute to wildfires and we are experiencing the most forest fires in history. The effects on the environment are reversible but efforts to put into policies and correctives have been resisted, slowed, and even prevented by economic interests and political opposition. The impact of climate change has physical and mental health issues as well. Increased respiratory and cardiovascular disease and premature death are all related to drastically changing and extreme weather conditions as well as waterborne and infectious diseases. I need not spend much time here listing the faults of big oil and the dangers of climate change. They are readily available with a minimum search. Here is the blunt fact: the generation in charge of the political, economic, social, and environmental decisions of the past century has failed to confront climate change in any significant way. If past behavior is the best predictor of future behavior, then a prediction that this generation will come to its senses and do anything significant about effective policies and strategies to address the dangers of global warming and climate change is unlikely. "It's time for the fossil fuel industry to stop lying to the American people and finally take serious steps to reduce emissions and address the global climate crisis they helped create" (House Oversight Committee Chair Carolyn Maloney told CNN in a statement). So that is why climate change is one of the four challenges I give to the coming generation.

It is no secret that we have experienced one of the most threatening health issues in history. In 1918, the "Spanish Flu" infected an estimated 500 million people worldwide. More than 50 million died all across the globe with 675,000 dying in the United States. It is estimated that about 500 million people or one-third of the world's population became infected with this virus. Beginning in 2020 COVID-19 accounted for 41 million cases and more than 1 million deaths across the globe. This pandemic is the worst in more than 100 years according to Dr. Anthony Fauci, Director of the National Institute of Allergy and Infectious Diseases. It ranks as one of the seven deadliest plagues in human history. Some people say that the last human being on earth will not die from an atomic blast but with a whimper – a moan as the virus infecting the body, at last, destroys its host. COVID-19 is considered the worst pandemic in American history surpassing the Flu epidemic of 1918. I consider it here because some epidemiologists believe that humans will increasingly have to face new deadly viruses. Our contact with insects, animals, and the presence of mutations in viruses globally will continue and increase. It climbs up the ladder of problems future generations will have to face to ensure our future on this planet.

So, a new generation of leaders, politicians, scientists, researchers, and educators inherit an earth with a set of issues and problems unsolved by previous generations. The past has set the agenda and with that agenda, we send our hopes that you are wiser than we have been.

EPILOGUE

A writing instructor some years ago told the class that there were three stages to informing an audience. Tell them what you are going to tell them; tell them; and, tell them what you told them. Or, introduction, body, and conclusion. It is time to tell you what I told you or, more formally, to give you the conclusion.

If you will permit me, I had a somewhat amusing (at least to me), thought about the span of this book. It covers the beginning of the universe, the formation of the earth, the development of our species, and our struggles with life right up to and including the present. Now if you think about it, that is 13.75 billion years. All this is in a few short pages. Quite an achievement! In those 13.75 billion years, what have we learned? Or, to be more connected to this endeavor, I was talking with an acquaintance and describing my hopes for publishing the book. After we had spoken for a while, he asked me, "Well, what are people going to take away from this book?" I told him that I was mainly writing it for our grandchildren, kind of like a letter from Grandpa. He said, "That's fine. What do you want them to take away from the book?" Kind of a pushy guy, but still something to think about.

My big answer is my hope is that as folks read this it will provoke thought. In fact, every chapter in this book began with a question or a thought that I wanted to spend more time with. Ideas and guesses become thoughts. Thoughts become sentences. Sentences become paragraphs. Paragraphs become chapters. Sometimes. Sometimes ideas and guesses become thoughts and that's it. They don't always make it to sentences and sentences don't always make it to paragraphs and so on. These are just the ones that did.

So just as I thought about these ideas, I am hopeful that you might too. I also hope that the thoughts in the book lead in the long run to a better, happier, and even richer life for you. That wish is personal for our grandchildren.

That's a global answer to the question of what I hope people take away. A bit more specific answer would go like this. "Thorns have Roses" is a metaphor. One of the lessons of life, for me, is that life comes complete with sadness, hard times, and even tragedy. One of the lessons of age is that those hard times aren't the end of the story. Even hard times sometimes, maybe even frequently, can end with happier outcomes than we first thought. I am so certain of this manly because I have lived a long time and my life has been, and continues to be an ongoing process of adapting to unexpected events that I had not planned on. Mostly small adaptations now, but in my life, I have maneuvered through some life crises. I said earlier that my dominant emotion in the present is gratitude. I mentioned that in my life crises, when the waves hit the rocky shore somehow they seemed to break my way. I attribute that to the people around me who gave me their support, some inner resilience, and, even, chance. More important than all of those is the attitude that life has a chance to work itself out.

"Put Me in Coach" carries the message that if life is going to work itself out, then you have to try. You have to get in the game (and again, pardon the sports metaphor).

Continuing with the sports metaphor and baseball. Don't look at a third strike. Swing the bat! Aside from sports, life isn't given to us. You have to try. The "Courage to be Imperfect" is a lesson that mistakes are nothing but one attempt at success. Wayne Gretzky is famous for saying, "You miss 100% of the shots you don't take." We have to try. Just look at a baby learning to walk. They fall down; they get up; they fall down; they get up; they fall down; they get up and on and on. They don't stop. They don't quit. It has been a very, very long time since I was a baby and so I don't really remember what I was thinking when I fell down all those times but I suspect this. I'll bet falling-down babies don't even know they are failing. They just taking the world as it is given and dealing with it. As a consequence, they learn to walk, run, jump, and go on in life to achieve amazing things!

People who do amazing things all seem to have certain qualities. Scientists have labeled those qualities "The Hardiness Factor." Just like the failing baby learning to walk, people with hardiness stick to it when tasks demand it. They, more often than not, aren't overwhelmed with life and see themselves as in control more often than not. It's not a 100% thing, but more often than not. Finally, when life knocks them down, they don't just get up. They get up with a working mind, looking for solutions that led to being knocked down in the first place. Mistakes, failures, and stumbles are information and it is possible to look at those as steps to the final success.

One of the ways to find an attitude of gratitude in the world is to recognize how simply lucky we are to be here at all. Out of the Big Bang, in the rough and tumble explosion that created the universe, somehow earth formed. It formed in such a way that organic life found a home. Ultimately, through planetary catastrophe, the little mammals crept out from under the rocks, and through one fortunate evolutionary step after another, we emerged. Everything had to be just right for us to be here (hence, "The Goldilocks Zone"). It is possible that out of personal catastrophes, we might carve out an "earth" home for ourselves and thus live a whole, peaceful, and, even, rich life. That is, of course, the source of gratitude.

It seems that so many people in our world look outside themselves for solutions to life's problems, issues, and dilemmas. Earlier, I noted that there is no shame in seeking help, especially when we need it. The flip side of that is that seeking help when we do not need it is a strategy for lifelong incompetence. I remember a statement from John F. Kennedy from long ago. He said, "God's work on earth is truly our own." Certainly, praying to God is no weakness if that is your belief. Yet, it may be a shortcoming if we do not remember as well to tend to the tasks that lie within our power. There is no challenge to faith to take care of the ordinary tasks of life. Just to follow up on that thought. While it may be true that "the path to Hell is paved with good intentions," it is certainly much more unlikely that "the path to Hell is paved with good acts." It seems to me that one way to find some comfort in what lies next for each of us is to live a decent life. It seems clear that every major religion, compassionate worldview, or philosophy of living includes the necessity of living with regard for others and even for the planet we live on.

I have said that the secret to a better world is straightforward. "Do more than your share" can start with a scrap of paper on the sidewalk but lead to a powerful local, national, or even world leader who models kindness, care, and responsibility. As I wrote in Chapter 11 – "Five Smooth Stones," Love, and Justice form the boundaries for a compassionate and caring world in which Hope, Courage, and Gratitude carry us through a rewarding life.

There are lessons in the ordinary events of life from which we can take some wisdom. Chapter 14 – "Two Ducks," is a short parable meant to teach that adult rules and structures must truly be necessary if we are not to trample the creativity and spontaneity of children. Living an honest, straight-ahead kind of life means that our biological nature and our learned style need to be reasonably compatible and that takes a long time to find the balance. Sometimes in life, we find people who are just so difficult to get along with, who imagine, create, and ignore the demonstrable teachings of life. The little parable "The Pig Who Thought He Was a Dog" is meant to teach that it is possible to live our life lives and let them live theirs. There is a line in Desiderata by Max Ehrmann that reads, "As far as possible without surrender be on good terms with all persons." It is sound advice. When I am in a less charitable mode, I might give the same advice a bit more harshly and say, as a comedian has said, "There's no cure for stupid." Just leave it alone. I hold that teachers are special people with special tasks. They are the guides for the next generation. The next generation is our future and we should teach them well. So wrote a short plea to the teachers of today for the children of tomorrow. Teach them so that they can love and be loved; work and be fulfilled. I have a hope that extends far into the future that we will continue to work to build a democratic world in which the worth and needs are all of us are met. I think the point to ponder in the preceding chapters leads readers to understand the worth of individuals, to not miss the gifts we have been given, to appreciate our place in the world, and to our commitment to and interdependence upon one another. I have said that I do not know with any certainty where we are going and what we will become. Yet, I do not fear the future. I am hopeful. I am hopeful because I do not know what lies ahead. The past is the parent of the present. The present is the parent of the future. We are making decisions now for the immediate future. The long-term future has a generation coming along who will make the decisions for that world. So, I have left some thoughts.

Thorns Have Roses

ABOUT THE AUTHOR

Ira David Welch was born in Memphis, Tennessee, in December 1940. Therein lies something of a story. My mother was born on December 7. As it happened, I made my appearance at 2:18 AM, and to my mother's displeasure, it was the morning of December 8. Back in those days, birth certificates were handwritten, and when the hospital staff filled in the birth date of December 8, she simply crossed it out and wrote December 7 since, I suppose, she figured that if she was going to go through all that effort, she should have a baby on her birthday! I celebrated my birthday on December 7 for most of my life. In fact, my driver's license, my military ID, and my passport all read December 7, 1940. I used a handwritten copy of my birth certificate, and all those agencies simply accepted it without question. It was not until I turned 65 and applied for Social Security that the actual date came to light. To qualify for Social Security, I had to submit an original copy of the birth certificate from the State of Tennessee. When it arrived, I was shocked to find I had been celebrating my birth on the wrong date for more than 65 years. That began a long process of changing all the public records such as Social Security, Medicare, and all my insurance and investment documents. Now, it is officially December 8, 1940. I am now in my 83rd year.

It has been a long and fruitful life. The truth of the matter is that I have lived longer and accomplished more than could have been expected. I come from an alcoholic family. My father and my brother were alcoholics, and so our family was shattered by secretiveness, violence, broken marriage, and meanness. It has been written that alcoholic families tend to be bi-modal so far as the children are concerned. One child will be an alcoholic and the other an overachiever. That was the case in our family. While my brother was the victim of alcoholism, the gene somehow missed me, and I became an overachiever. I have been fortunate to have accomplished more than my limited gifts would have predicted. My family of origin are all gone now. My mother died earlier than expected, I suppose in part because of the stresses of an alcoholic husband and son. My father and brother suffered from the effects of alcohol.

While I lost my family of origin, I have been blessed to live now in a nuclear family that includes my wife of more than 50 years and our two sons, David and Daniel. Both sons now have families of their own. David married Shauna Moser, and now they have a son, Aiden. Daniel married Alison Hatch, and they have two children, Paige and Ryan. It is difficult to express the meaning they have brought to my life.

Out of that alcoholic family, I managed to graduate from high school. After a year or two, I enlisted in the United States Army and grew to manhood during my military service. The army was a life-reassuring experience for me and led me to enter college, where I met educators who became mentors and into a career where I advanced and was successful. I obtained my bachelor's and master's degrees at what was then Colorado State College. Then, taught for a year before I entered my doctoral program at the University of Florida and received my doctoral degree in 1970. Over the years, I published several books and professional articles, and I was recognized as a Licensed Psychologist and was honored to be named a Diplomate by the American Board of Professional Psychology. I worked in two years as a preschool teacher. I taught at the University level for more than 40 years and retired as Professor Emeritus from the University of Northern Colorado in 1997. After retirement from UNC, I accepted some administrative positions across the country and ultimately retired as the Dean of the Graduate School of Professional Psychology of the University of St. Thomas in Minnesota. That was in 2007.

Now, 16 years after retirement, my wife, Marie and I live in Denver, Colorado and I continue to be physically active with golf and pickleball and intellectually alive with writing and an occasional speech or presentation before various groups, the most notable of which are Unitarian-Universalist churches. My youngest son, Daniel, and I publish children's books together under the pen name of Daniel Davidson, and that has been a source of great satisfaction to me. This book combines some of the speeches I have given to UU churches across the country as well as additional chapters on thoughts and stories that have meaning to me and which I hope will touch and perhaps guide the lives of others.

Made in the USA
Columbia, SC
16 January 2025